STROMATOLITES

Ancient, Beautiful, and Earth-Altering

Bob Leis | Bruce L. Stinchcomb | Illustrations by Terry McKee

4880 Lower Valley Road • Atglen, PA 19310

Other Schiffer books on related subjects:

A Collector's Guide to Granite Pegmatites, Vandall T. King, 978-0-7643-3578-5

Collecting Fluorescent Minerals, Stuart Schneider, 978-0-7643-3619-5

Cenozoic Fossils 1: Paleogene, Bruce L. Stinchcomb, 978-0-7643-3424-5

Cenozoic Fossils 2: The Neogene, Bruce L. Stinchcomb, 978-0-7643-3580-8

Type set in Bell MT/ITC Souvenir

ISBN: 978-0-7643-4897-6
Printed in China

Published by Schiffer Publishing, Ltd.
4880 Lower Valley Road
Atglen, PA 19310
Phone: (610) 593-1777; Fax: (610) 593-2002
E-mail: Info@schifferbooks.com

For our complete selection of fine books on this and related subjects, please visit our website at www.schifferbooks.com. You may also write for a free catalog.

This book may be purchased from the publisher. Please try your bookstore first.

We are always looking for people to write books on new and related subjects. If you have an idea for a book, please contact us at proposals@schifferbooks.com.

Schiffer Publishing's titles are available at special discounts for bulk purchases for sales promotions or premiums. Special editions, including personalized covers, corporate imprints, and excerpts can be created in large quantities for special needs. For more information, contact the publisher.

Dedication

More than half of the fossil stromatolites presented in this book are of Precambrian age. Prior to the 1970s, geologists questioned the biogenicity of structures known as stromatolites. That is because some stromatolites occurred in rocks dating to billions of years ago and many believed it unlikely that life could be this ancient. Stanley Tyler and Gene LaBerge's discovery of undoubted microfossils in stromatolites in the two-billion-year-old Gunflint Iron Formation in the 1950s, which was announced to the scientific world in 1954 (Tyler and Barghoorn, Science 1954), proved that these ancient stromatolites indeed were biogenic and established a whole new field of science—paleomicrobiology. Without the dedicated fieldwork of Gene LaBerge and his mentor, Stanley Tyler, the objects that grace these pages would be considered scientifically insignificant. With this in mind, we dedicate this book to Gene LaBerge of Oshkosh, Wisconsin.

Contents

Preface

R. J. Leis

Seventeen years ago, while rummaging through the fossil section of the Enchanted Garden rock shop in Richfield, Minnesota, I discovered something that led me to write this book. What I found was a small slab of polished rock that had a very pleasing look. I turned it over to read the information taped to the back of the slab. It read "Mary Ellen Jasper—Algae Iron Formation Minnesota—1.8 Billion Yrs. Old (one of the oldest fossils)." When I noted the 1.8 billion years ago (b.y.a.), I thought, "Wow! How can I be holding something that old?" I purchased the slab for $19 and took it home. A little research told me that I had bought a fossilized stromatolite. I also learned that 1.8 b.y.a. stromatolites are not even that old; geologically, there are much older ones out there.

I was hooked. Before finding the slab of Mary Ellen Jasper I had developed a casual interest in all types of fossils. I didn't focus on any one kind, so I would collect a trilobite here or a brachiopod there or whatever looked cool. But since discovering that stromatolite, my focus has remained on stromatolites, or rocks of stromatolitic and biogenic origin.

My business card states, in bold letters with an exclamation mark, that "Pond Scum Rules!" It is my hope that after reading this book you will know why I think this lowly life form rules, and that you will have an appreciation for stromatolites and all they have provided us over vast spans of geologic time. My card also notes that I am an avid admirer/collector of stromatolites, algal mats, and generally

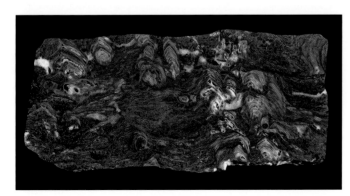

My first stromatolite

all rocks of stromatolitic and biogenic origin. Nowhere on that card do I state that I am a geologist—nor do I pretend to be one. I am just someone who really, really enjoys collecting, admiring, and learning about stromatolites.

When I began looking into stromatolites, I could not find a single book written for someone without a geologic background. There is a lot of technical literature out there written by PhDs. I am sure the information presented in these papers is useful, but it is far beyond what was helpful to a novice collector like me.

The closest understandable book I could find was Dr. Bruce Stinchcomb's *World's Oldest Fossils* (Schiffer Publishing, 2007). His book is excellent and would be a great companion to this one, but it is not devoted entirely to stromatolites and did not answer all my questions. So I set out to provide a resource for those who collect and admire these beautiful, fascinating objects. I do not claim the information presented is the latest or last word, and there are technical matters that will not be addressed, but I hope that after reading the book, you will want to have at least one stromatolite in your fossil collection. For it was stromatolites and their photosynthetic moneran "cousins" that altered the earth and enabled multi-celled organisms to advance.

Some people in academia and elsewhere look down on fossil collecting and feel it should be left to the "professionals." I disagree. Stromatolites can be very beautiful when cut and polished; they are educational and link us to the distant past. They also are priced relatively reasonably compared to other fossils. Looking for stromatolites can get us outdoors to enjoy nature, and an amateur may even enhance science by discovering new material. Methods for collecting stromatolites will be presented later in the book.

Before we can begin collecting fossilized specimens, we should have an understanding of what stromatolites are and how they are formed. You will note I am not referring to stromatolites in the past tense because they are still growing and proliferating in secluded corners of the world. Though not as numerous as they used to be, they are still in existence, unlike a lot of other fossilized plants or animals (e.g. dinosaurs) that are extinct.

Introduction

R. J. Leis

Buried deep in the past and enduring to this day are the most remarkable organisms that ever existed. They are responsible for the structures known as stromatolites—communities of microorganisms that altered Earth and allowed evolution to proceed.

To appreciate stromatolites, a little history of Earth is in order. Please examine the two illustrations at the end of this introduction. The earth is approximately 4.6 billion years old, which is as accurate as can be determined using radiometric age dating measurements, a method that appears to be well established.

The first 800 million years of Earth's history consisted of the Hadean Era, which refers to the hell-like conditions on earth at this time. Earth contained no free oxygen and

Figure 01. Inside this slab of rock are crystals of zircon more than 4.4 billion years old. This material dates back to within 200 million years of when Earth formed. The sediment containing the zircon is approximately 3 billion years old and comes from the Jack Hills region of Western Australia.

most of its surface was molten, with a lot of volcanism and meteor bombardments. Earth's atmosphere contained high levels of carbon dioxide and methane, which, combined with the extreme temperatures, precluded any life forms.

Sometime around 800 million years (m.y.) after the earth formed, its surface cooled so that what was partially a liquid began to change to a solid. Solid rock formed, preserving the record of the planet. These rocks, just shy of 4 billion years old, ushered in the Archean Era.

The Archean Era lasted approximately from 4 b.y.a. to 2.5 b.y.a. Archean means ancient, and it was during this time that life may have begun. How did life on earth begin? I'll leave that question up to the others, however it's a big question with profound consequences—if it can ever be answered. What's important is that somehow life did begin in its simplest form, anaerobic (non-oxygen-using) one-celled bacteria. These prokaryotic life forms are the predecessors to all life on Earth today. Prokaryotes are single-celled organisms that lack a cell nucleus. Prokaryotes in the kingdom Monera include the domains of Archaea (archaebacteria-ancient bacteria) and Bacteria (eubacteria-true bacteria). The archaebacteria are the most tolerant, with some able to live in extremely hostile environments such as thermal vents. Presently their descendants are called extremophiles. Archaebacteria (thought by some to be a separate kingdom) consist of a group of prokaryotes known as methanogens, halophiles, and some chemosynthetic bacteria. Eubacteria include the blue-green algae known as cyanobacteria, the organisms usually responsible for stromatolites.

Some organisms of the Archean Era became colonial. Approximately 3.5 b.y.a. cyanobacteria began to form mats

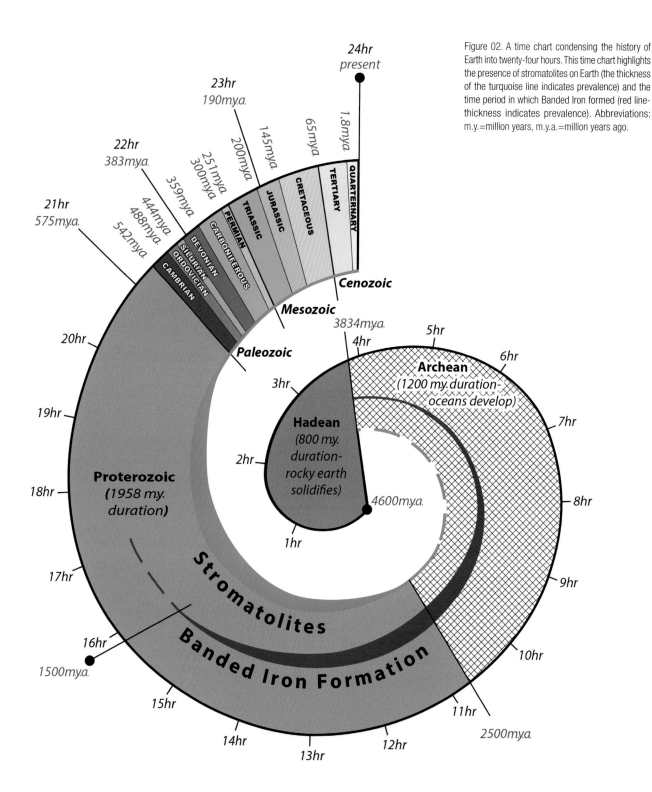

Figure 02. A time chart condensing the history of Earth into twenty-four hours. This time chart highlights the presence of stromatolites on Earth (the thickness of the turquoise line indicates prevalence) and the time period in which Banded Iron formed (red line-thickness indicates prevalence). Abbreviations: m.y.=million years, m.y.a.=million years ago.

or "colonies" that became the basis of "my amazing" stromatolites. The earliest concrete evidence of stromatolites is 3.4–3.5 b.y.a. in Archean Era rocks in what is known as the Pilbara Block in Western Australia. This includes the well-known Strelley Pool stromatolites. Cyanobacteria evolved and generated their own food and energy using sunlight through the process of photosynthesis. The oxygen produced by these early photosynthetic colonial bacteria oxidized the

ferrous iron dissolved in the oceans. Atmospheric oxygen did not rise to any significant level during the Archean Era.

The geologic third time period we will address is the Proterozoic Era that lasted from 2.5 b.y.a. until 535 million years ago (m.y.a.). This is the time period when the first stable continents appeared. It was also during this time that fossils appear in abundance, these being mostly stromatolites—Archean stromatolites are rare. Approximately 2.9–1.9

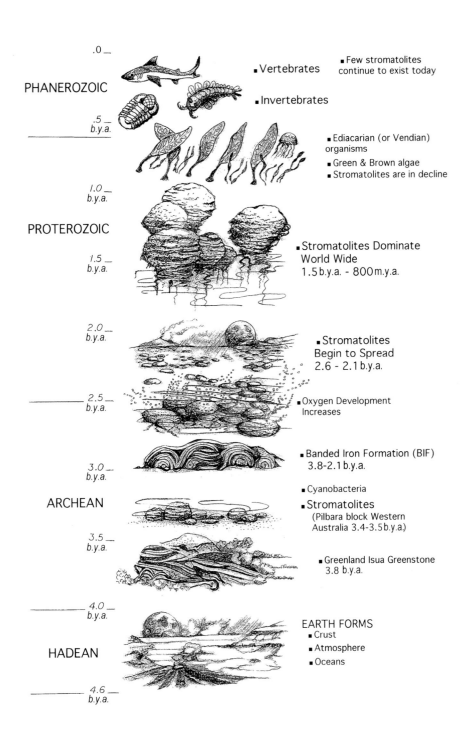

PHANEROZOIC

.0 —

.5 —
b.y.a.

- Vertebrates

- Invertebrates

- Few stromatolites
  continue to exist today

- Ediacarian (or Vendian)
  organisms
- Green & Brown algae
- Stromatolites are in decline

PROTEROZOIC

1.0 —
b.y.a.

1.5 —
b.y.a.

- Stromatolites Dominate
  World Wide
  1.5 b.y.a. - 800 m.y.a.

2.0 —
b.y.a.

2.5 —
b.y.a.

- Stromatolites
  Begin to Spread
  2.6 - 2.1 b.y.a.

- Oxygen Development
  Increases

ARCHEAN

3.0 —
b.y.a.

3.5 —
b.y.a.

- Banded Iron Formation (BIF)
  3.8-2.1 b.y.a.

- Cyanobacteria

- Stromatolites
  (Pilbara block Western
  Australia 3.4-3.5 b.y.a.)

- Greenland Isua Greenstone
  3.8 b.y.a.

HADEAN

4.0 —
b.y.a.

4.6 —
b.y.a.

EARTH FORMS
- Crust
- Atmosphere
- Oceans

Figure 03. An illustrated timeline of the early Earth with
emphasis on stromatolites.

b.y.a. we see the first evidence of oxygen build-up in the atmosphere. By 1.8 b.y.a., along with the infusion of oxygen into the atmosphere, the first multi-celled (eukaryotic) organisms may have appeared. Stromatolites increased both in number and diversity through most of the Proterozoic Era, then they began to decline in abundance and diversity about 700 m.y.a. Although living stromatolites exist today, stromatolite fossils are much less common after about 450 m.y.a.

Interestingly, as old as fossilized stromatolites can be, they were not confirmed by science as evidence of early living organisms until the 1960s.

It is our hope that this book will help readers understand what a stromatolite is and what they have meant to our very existence. In addition, numerous photos will exhibit the diversity and beauty of stromatolites.

Chapter One

What Are Stromatolites?

R. J. Leis

When I first obtained a slab of stromatolite, all I knew at the time was that it was pretty and also very old. When I began to look into what stromatolites were I began to find out that they were much more. Finding understandable information about stromatolites was not easy. We hope this chapter will answer in an understandable way what stromatolites are along with their various types and morphologies.

When I looked up the dictionary definition of stromatolites I found the following: 1) German term stromatolith coined by Ernest Kalkowsky in 1908 from the Greek words *stroma* meaning bed, mattress, or layer, and *lithos* meaning stone; 2) Laminated organo-sedimentary structures formed by microbial trapping and binding of sediments or precipitation of dissolved minerals; 3) Structure consisting of laminated carbonate or silicate rocks produced over geological time by trapping, binding, or precipitating of sediment by groups of microorganisms, primarily cyanobacteria; 4) A rocky mass consisting of layers of calcareous material and sediment bound by the prolific growth of cyanobacteria.

The dictionary really didn't help much when I initially sought to understand what a stromatolite is. However, now that I know more about them, the dictionary definitions do make sense.

When I began collecting fossils as a hobby, I assumed that the fossilized stromatolites I was finding in the market were fossils. I was soon to discover that in 99.9 percent of the cases stromatolites are not actual fossils, but rather trace fossils. A trace fossil records ecological interactions, but not the preservation of body fossils. The actual organisms responsible for the formation of the stromatolite rarely are preserved. In some rare cases the stromatolites were infiltrated with mineral solutions, a process that preserved the organisms that actually built the structure, but this is rare. A fossilized stromatolite could be looked upon as a building that has been buried for millions of years. The structure is there but its inhabitants are long gone. A fossilized stromatolite, nevertheless, is evidence of former life.

Scientists assume that before stromatolites formed there were single-celled bacteria existing in aquatic environments. At some point the single-celled bacteria combined to form colonial bacteria, which eventually led to various types of stromatolite formations. Stromatolites can also be referred to as a type of microbialite because they are influenced by microbial growth when they form.

Modern stromatolites involve all three recognized super kingdoms: 1) Bacteria; 2) Archaea (non-oxygen bacteria), and 3) Eukarya (cells with a nucleus, as is the case with true algae). Ancient stromatolites were almost exclusively bacterial. Modern stromatolites have both photosynthetic bacteria sharing with algae (a eukaryote), the latter which had not yet evolved in the Archean Era.

Living stromatolites have a green layer of cyanobacteria, usually 1 mm (0.04 inch), on the top that use light for photosynthesis. This layer is sheet-like and has a sticky slime, which is secreted by its cells and also makes cyanobacteria-coated rocks so slippery. This slimy substance is what holds the mat together. Just below the green layer is a thin zone made up of green sulfur and purple photosynthetic bacteria that are able to absorb wavelengths of light passing through the cyanobacteria layer. We will call this the purple zone. This zone requires anoxic conditions for photosynthesis and cannot thrive in environments containing free oxygen. The green layer and purple zone

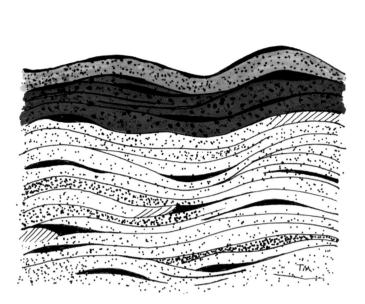

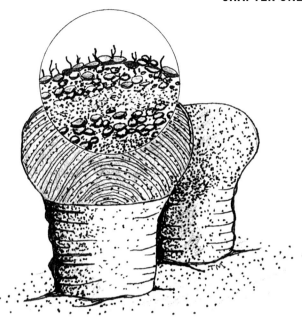

Figure 1-01. This illustrates, in a greatly enhanced way, the green and purple photosynthetic food producing part of a stromatolite. These green and purple zones are underlaid by an oxygen-depleted zone that consumes organic matter produced by the stromatolite's top two layers.

Figure 1-02. Illustrated section of a stromatolite exhibiting the layering and cyanobacterial strands that trap sediment. Calcium carbonate will cement the trapped sediment, resulting in the characteristic stromatolitic laminations.

produce food by photosynthetic processes using carbon dioxide and sunlight. Below the purple zone are oxygen-depleted layers consisting of anaerobic bacteria and Archea. Archea are prokaryotic microorganisms because, like bacteria, they lack a cell nucleus, but they are distinguished from bacteria by their DNA and are often found in hostile environments such as volcanic vents and hot springs. The organic matter produced by the top two layers is consumed by the oxygen-depleted zone, which also produces sulfur as a by-product.

The primary producers, cyanobacteria (green layer) are the architects of the stromatolite. Cyanobacteria are constantly growing and many forms of cyanobacteria calcify, forming a calcium carbonate superstructure, which is what is preserved in a fossil stromatolite. Layers of mucus form over mats of the cyanobacterial cells, and debris becomes trapped in this mucus. All of this can be cemented together by calcium carbonate to grow thin laminations of limestone. The laminations accumulate over time (sometimes thousands of years) to result in the banded patterns common to fossilized stromatolites. These layers, or laminations, are formed by the combination of calcification and trapped sediment, material deposited with the tides or other disturbances, as stromatolites are generally found in shallow oceans, lagoons, hot springs, or freshwater lakes.

Cyanobacteria and bacteria from the purple zone are constantly growing upward, striving for sunlight. When conditions are static, the growth surface is static, the mat remains unchanged and no new layers are added. However, if events such as tides, floods, or perhaps dust hit the growth surface, the cyanobacteria and purple zones respond. The cyanobacteria and purple zones will move upward through the debris to find a new sunny surface they can colonize. The anaerobes move up from below to feed on the remaining dead organic matter created as new layers are formed.

Laminations or layers are indicators of an incremental depositing process in which an occasional or periodic change of process or interference results in discrete, laterally continuous layers. Layers appear in a variety of morphologies: flat, domal, columnar, or conical. These layers usually have a distinct signature that enables someone familiar with stromatolites to distinguish them from layers produced by non-biogenic processes.

Laminations usually are convex upward. Stromatolites are sorted by their growth type, and as long as the calcium carbonate structure remains unbroken and laminar, it remains a stromatolite regardless of whether the stromatolite is flat, domal, columnar, or conical.

Most stromatolites can be found in five major classes or morphological stromatolite structures. The first one is the flat-layered or planar stromatolite sometimes called Stratifera. The second and most common type of stromatolite is the domal form, which grow in gently bowing concentric layers. These may also be called Cryptozoan-type stromatolites. The third type of stromatolite is a columnar type that may branch into long finger-like structures (digitate) and also may be known as Collenia-type. The fourth type consists of conical stromatolites known as Conophyton. The fifth type are the thrombolites, a more complicated stromatolite as they may appear unlaminated on the surface, but when examined internally are vaguely laminated. The thrombolites' laminae may become absent, missed, vague, or mottled due to the result of powerful tides and being subject to grazing, which breaks the fabric. The thrombolite reacts to the broken fabric by filling in the void with calcium carbonate, causing a distinctive patchy look instead of smooth, even layering. When examined, fossilized thrombolites often look as though an explosion has occurred. Thrombolites are often formed by a mixed bacterial and eukaryotic community. The eukaryotes are algae, the simplest of plants. Unlike the cyanobacteria, which deposits calcium carbonate in a relatively linear fashion, algae grows in long strands. Some of the algae precipitates a calcium carbonate tube and grows faster than the cyanobacteria, which also contributes to the mottled look of the thrombolites.

Figure 1-04. Stromatolitic chert, Gasconade formation, Lower Ordovician, St. Robert, Missouri. This specimen illustrates exceptionally flat or planar laminations not often seen in stromatolites.

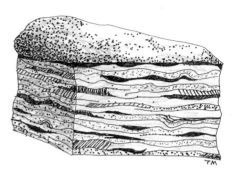

Figure 1-03. Depiction of a flat, planar stromatolite, sometimes also referred to as *Stratifera*. The laminations exhibited in flat stromatolites are fairly level, slightly wavy, or wrinkled.

Figure 1-05. Stromatolite from the Lykins Formation, Permian, N.W. Boulder County, Boulder, Colorado. This *Stratifera*, or flat specimen, exhibits the more typical wavy laminations found in this type of morphology.

Figure 1-07. Kona Dolomite, Chocolay group, Chocolay Hills, Northern Michigan, 2.2 b.y.a. Another *Stratifera* stromatolite from a formation that typically yields domal specimens.

Figure 1-06. A *Stratifera* stromatolite from Tower Soudan Mine, 2.5 b.y.a., St. Louis County, Minnesota. Normally stromatolites from this formation are columnar in morphology, but this specimen shows that there can be more than one morphology from the same formation. The difference in morphology is likely influenced by the depth of the ocean in which it formed.

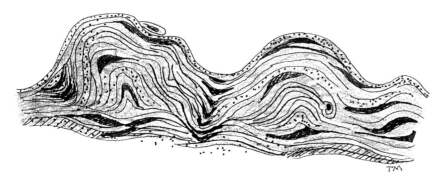

Figure 1-08. Domal stromatolite, a type of stromatolite that formed in a relatively deep offshore environment. This type of stromatolite is generally more massive, rounded, and not columnar-like. The mounds may be composed of large quantities of digitate stromatolites. Domal stromatolites are often referred to as *Cryptozoan*.

Figure 1-09. Stromatolite from the Cotter Formation, Taney County, Cedar Creek, Missouri, Lower Ordovician. Front (cut) and back (uncut) photos of vertically cut domal form of stromatolite showing the bowing concentric layers typical in this type of morphology.

Figure 1-10. Oneota Formation, Oconto County, Wisconsin, Lower Ordovician. A good example of a domal stromatolite, front (cut) and back (uncut); also called *Cryptozoan*.

Figure 1-11. R. Leis and Bob Weikert viewing the large domal stromatolite near Grandview, Wisconsin. This stromatolite was carried by glaciers about five miles from where it originated in a large mass of Bad River Dolomite domes in Bayfield County, Wisconsin, and is approximately 2.3 billion years old.

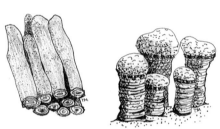

Figure 1-12. Drawing of columnar stromatolites showing that they can be solitary or clustered. The columns can vary in shape and size and may be branching or non-branching. These types of columnar stromatolites may also be referred to as collenial or digitate. Columnar stromatolites may be club shaped or narrowing upwards or they may have a narrow base and widen upward. They are formed by convex upward laminations.

Figure 1-13. Cluster of digitate columnar-type stromatolites. Figure on right is as one might find them in the field on a bed of non-stromatolitic matrix. Figure on left is what it might look like if the cluster on the right were cut into a cube.

Figure 1-14. Stromatolite from Russia, Precambrian. An excellent example of a columnar stromatolite, also referred to as digitate.

Figure 1-15. Mary Ellen Jasper, *Collenia undosa*, Biwabik Formation, St. Louis County, Minnesota, 1.8–1.9 b.y.a. Another digitate form of columnar stromatolite. Note how some of the digits on this stromatolite are branched.

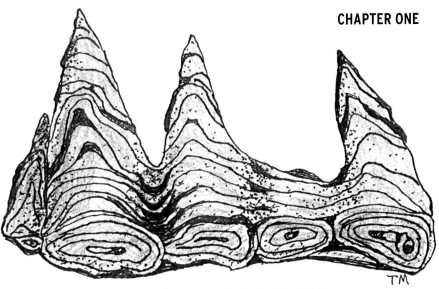

Figure 1-16. Drawing of a *Conophyton* or conical morphology. This drawing illustrates that in this type of stromatolite the laminations are vertically stacked inside each other and usually have a distinct cone or peak upward.

Figure 1-17. Mary Ellen Jasper, *Collenia undosa*, Biwabik Formation, St. Louis County, Minnesota, 1.8–1.9 b.y.a. A columnar stromatolite shows the digitate stromatolites cut horizontally, exhibiting the bull's eye appearance obtained by cutting the stromatolite in this way.

Figure 1-18. Mary Ellen Jasper, *Collenia undosa*, Biwabik Iron Formation. Mary Ellen mine, St. Louis County, Minnesota, 1.8–1.9 b.y.a. An interesting slab that appears to show digitate stromatolite changing to conical.

Figure 1-19. *Conophyton* sp., a slab of stromatolite from the Eminence Formation, Upper Cambrian. Shown are the cone-inside-a-cone structure and pointed laminae. This stromatolite is found occasionally through the Ozarks of Missouri and is thought to have formed in geothermal springs near what is now Womack, Missouri.

Figure 1-20. Russian stromatolite, *Gionophytum gargarnicus*, Riphaen Formation, Upper river, Bakson village of Bakson, Eastern Sayan, Russia, Precambrian. An excellent example of a *Conophyton* morphology stromatolite.

Figure 1-21. *Conophyton* stromatolite of unknown age, collected on the beach at Prince William Island, Alaska.

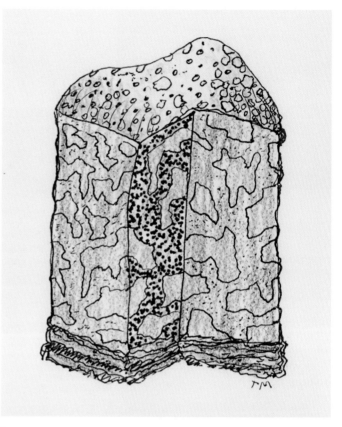

Figure 1-22. Drawing of thrombolites showing the broken or clotted laminae. Thrombolites form similarly to other stromatolites but their laminations are not intact. Much is yet to be known about how these structures form. Some still question whether thrombolites are unique structures or disrupted stromatolites.

Figure 1-23. Thrombolites are still forming today. This is a large thrombolite formation at Lake Clifton, approximately 12.5 miles south of Perth, Australia.

Figure 1-24. Thrombolite stromatolite from Fremont County, Colorado, Jurassic in age. Two half-pieces showing the broken laminae and explosive appearance so commonly seen in this type of fossilized stromatolite.

Paleocene era and collected
shows its carpet-like structure
carpet.

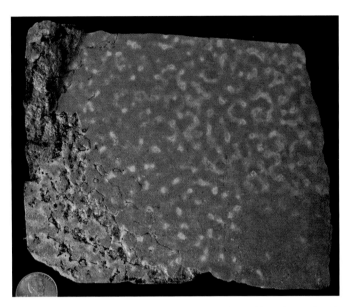

Figure 1-26. Moneran mat, Cope Hollow Formation, Reynolds County, Missouri, approximately 1.5 b.y. old. Polished slab of moneran mat illustrating alternating sequence of monerans and ash fall.

n rates and locations
jor factors affecting
y. The domal-type
far offshore, the flat-
the shore, and the
s between the flat and
indicate a striving for
debris deposits. They
geothermal) conditions.
hia, Conophyton and
omatolites. There are,
re similar in composition
hough technically they
as stromatolitic.
s similar in composition
mat. It is a bacterial
nthetic cyanobacteria at
cteria in the middle, and
m. The main difference,
es not calcify. These are
as a result of having no
e horizontally and do not
nade by true stromatolites.
irely
a on
ather-
pick
p like
a carpet. Moneran m_____ row in
lakes, oceans, salt lakes, and puddles,
and in hot or cold conditions. Moneran
mats can also form wherever it is moist,
and can hold on to surfaces so well
that thin moneran mats may have
ripple marks, mud cracks, raindrop

Figure 1-27. Rough piece of mottled-moneran mat from volcanic ash beds of western Reynolds County, Missouri, approximately 1.5 b.y. old.

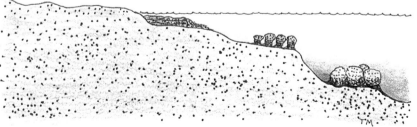

Figure 1-28. Illustration showing where various stromatolite morphologies may form in relation to water depth. One must keep in mind that there are lots of variables that determine stromatolite morphology; water depth is only one variable, but an important one.

impressions and even impressions of plants and animals. The peculiar Ediacaran fossils of the latest Precambrian Era appear to be associated with such moneran mats.

Another stromatolitic formation is the oncolite. Oncolites are similar to stromatolites, but instead of forming columns they form spherical structures. Oncolites are essentially round cyanobacteria balls, some of which are sometimes referred to as *Girvanella*. There are three types of oncolites: dynamic, static, and dynamic-static type. The dynamic oncolite exists in environments with constant current, or tides. This action rolls them about, causing sediments and carbonate sands to stick to the cyanobacteria surface; the cyanobacteria will then sprout tubes through the carbonate layer and colonize the new surface. They will then repeat the process, causing concentric layers of cyanobacteria, algae, and carbonate. The static type can resemble a sponge, and these grow today in northern Mexico. This type may have a Collenia undulation surface radiating around a central nucleus, but not always; these grow in waters that have a slow current. The third type, as the name suggests, is a mix of the two. The dynamic-static type starts off in currents rolling in tight concentric layers, and then, when deposited into quieter waters, will begin to radiate Collenia type fingers.

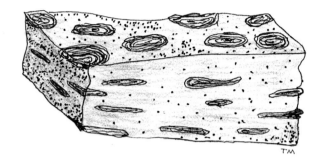

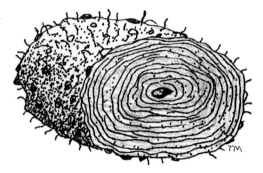

Figure 1-29. Drawing of an individual algal ball or oncolite cut as a cross section showing the laminations. This is an illustration of a dynamic-type oncolite. The top drawing illustrates what oncolites might look like in matrix.

Figure 1-30. Pisolitic Limestone from the Tansill Formation, Eddy County, New Mexico, Permian. This slab is an excellent example of a dynamic oncolite. Their packed appearance is probably due to wave or tidal action causing a concentration of oncolites.

Figure 1-31. Slab of dynamic-type oncolite from the Salina Formation, Wood County, Ohio; Upper Silurian in age. The slab has been cut and polished perpendicularly to the individual nodules and clearly exhibits the multi-colored growth rings.

Figure 1-32. Freshwater stromatolite, Lady of Angels Lake, near Ascension, State of Chihuahua, Mexico, Upper Cretaceous. This oncolite formed around a rhyolite nucleus and the collenia-like undulated surface is clearly evident. This is a static-type oncolite.

Figure 1-33. Oncolite, Flagstaff Formation, Sanpete County, Thistle, Utah, Paleocene. Another static-type oncolite that used a gastropod, *Oxytrema* sp., as a nucleus. This particular specimen shows growth rings around the nucleus that are not collenial-like but much more laminar.

Figure 1-34. The oncolites featured in figures 33–35 formed approximately 58–66 m.y.a. in a large body of water known as Lake Flagstaff, which covered large sections of northeast and central Utah and is part of the Green River Formation. This specimen formed around a snail, *Oreoconus* sp. The collenial-type laminations are evident upon close examination.

Figure 1-35. A block of material commonly known as bird's-eye marble in matrix. This material came from the same location described in figures 33 and 34. These bird's-eye features were formed by freely moving stromatolites that grew around gastropods, snails, clams, twigs, or other debris. The algae used these objects as a nucleus similar to the way stromatolites used wood (presented in Chapter 9) as a nucleus to form their distinctive concentric shapes.

Figure 1-36. *Somphosongia* sp., Burlingame Limestone, Jackson County, Kansas, Pennsylvanian in age. Photo of the third type of oncolite that is a mix of dynamic and static. At one time this specimen was an oncolite with tight concentric layers. Upon being deposited in quieter waters, distinctive *Collenia* digitate "fingers" formed, as exhibited in the slab.

Figure 1-37. Brecciated stromatolite from the Oneota Formation, Buffalo County, Wisconsin, Ordovician. The angular and broken fragments of stromatolite are clearly evident in this specimen. The original stromatolitic structures were shattered into irregular shapes, probably in the surf, and then buried under the stromatolite colonies that subsequently grew above.

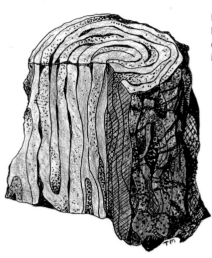

Figure 1-38. This drawing shows how different the same stromatolite can look depending on whether it is cut vertically or horizontally.

Figure 1-39. Mary Ellen Jasper, *Collenia undosa*, Biwabik Iron Formation. Mary Ellen Mine, St. Louis County, Minnesota, 1.8–1.9 b.y.a. This piece of digitate Mary Ellen Jasper is cut both vertically and horizontally. If the piece is cut vertically you see the long digitate stromatolites. If the piece is cut horizontally you have a bull's eye look at the same columnar or digitate stromatolite. Same piece, very different appearance.

You may encounter a brecciated fossilized stromatolite on your stromatolite journey. The definition of breccia is a rock composed of angular fragments embedded in a fine grain matrix. Breccia can occur as a result of explosive ejections, plate tectonics, meteorite impact, or wave activity. Breccia differs from conglomerate in that the fragments are angular instead of rounded.

When it comes to brecciated stromatolites, the brecciation is most often the result of wave or surf activity. In most cases it is thought that the original stromatolite was shattered into irregular shapes, most likely by surf, then buried under stromatolite colonies that grew above them.

Slabs of fossilized stromatolites can look very different depending on whether they are cut horizontally or vertically. For example, a columnal or digitate stromatolite cut horizontally will give you a rounded or "bull's eye"

appearance. If the same stromatolite is cut vertically, you will see the columns or digitates lengthwise. Same stromatolite, very different look.

The colors of stromatolites can vary greatly due to the billions or millions of years in which various minerals have percolated through stromatolite-bearing formations. Different mineral solutions impact different colors such as the greens from copper or the reds from hematite. A mixture of minerals can result in unusual and beautifully colored stromatolites.

As to the age of fossilized stromatolites, geologists primarily depend on the strata in which they occur. The age of the stromatolite strata is determined by its relative position and relationship to other strata. Radiometric age dating may be needed in determining the age of some rock strata. Age dating of stromatolites and other fossils is not easily explained and can be rather complex. As a nonprofessional I rely on the age information provided by the sellers. When I collect stromatolites I record where the specimen comes from and then talk to geologists or read articles on the Internet to help age it. Without this information, your stromatolite becomes just another pretty rock.

There is a lot yet to be learned. Living and fossilized stromatolites vary to such an extent that they can be difficult to categorize or narrow down. Most fossils, such as trilobites, have distinct shapes that can be quantified, but stromatolites do not necessarily have this. Many educated guesses are involved when trying to interpret what one is looking at in the fossil record. For more information, the paper "Stromatolites: Biogenicity, Biosignatures, and Bioconfusion" does an excellent job of addressing stromatolite confusion and ambiguity (Awramik and Grey 2005). I am sure much more will become known about stromatolites and especially fossil stromatolites, but for now we will have to use our best assumptions.

Glossary

Anaerobe. Any of various organisms, almost all prokaryotes, that do not require oxygen for growth and perform their functions better in the absence of oxygen.

Anoxic. The complete absence of dissolved molecular oxygen (O_2).

Archaea or Archeobacteria. A kingdom or domain of single-celled microorganisms. They have no cell nucleus like other prokaryotes, but they have unique metabolic properties that separate them from bacteria. Archaea are one of three categories of life; the other two are bacteria and eukaryotes.

Archaeans. Diverse microbes of the Archaea kingdom.

b.y.a. Billion years ago.

Calcareous. Rocks and other earth materials that have an abundance of calcium carbonate ($CaCO_3$).

Calcification. A hardening or solidifying by deposition of calcium or calcium salts such as calcium carbonate.

Calcium carbonate. A descriptive term used for rocks and other materials that have an abundance of the chemical compound with the formula $CaCO_3$, an example being limestone.

Collenia. A convex, slightly arched stromatolite produced by late Precambrian blue-green algae of the genus Collenia, one of the five types of stromatolite morphology.

Colonial bacteria. A cluster of bacteria growing on the surface or within a solid medium.

Conophyton. Stromatolite morphology that is cone-shaped.

Convex. Having a surface that is curved or rounded outward.

Cryptozoan. Stromatolite morphology that is domal.

Cryptozoon. Name given to fossils found near Saratoga Springs, New York, by James Hall (Hall 1883). It means hidden animal.

Cyanobacteria. A prokaryotic microorganism capable of oxygen-producing photosynthesis (previously classified and commonly termed blue-green algae).

Ediacaran. Soft-bodied, many-celled marine organisms of the Precambrian era, thought to be the oldest known multicellular form of life.

Eukaryote. Any organism whose cells contain a nucleus and other organelle structures enclosed within membranes, one of the three kingdoms or domains of life.

Geothermal. Heat from the earth's interior.

Girvanella. A genus of fossil algae characterized by microscopic tubular filaments identified in some oncolites.

Laminae. A fine layer as a part of stromatolite structure.

Matrix. The solid material in which something is embedded such as the natural rock that holds fossils.

Microbialite. Geologic or stone structure produced by biogenic activity of numerous microorganisms, which usually involves photosynthesis.

Monerans. Any organism of the taxonomic kingdom Monera, single-celled organisms that reproduce by splitting in two (binary fission) and have no cell nucleus; a kingdom of life in which all members are prokaryotes.

Photosynthesis. A metabolic process carried out by photosynthetic bacteria, cyanobacteria, algae, and plants in which light energy is converted to chemical energy and stored in molecules of carbohydrates.

Prokaryote. Microorganisms with a membrane and cell wall but no nucleus. Prokaryotic cells may have photosynthetic pigments, such as those found in cyanobacteria.

Rhyolite. An igneous volcanic rock with a silica-rich composition.

Stratifera. Stromatolite morphology that is flat or slightly wavy.

Bibliography

Awramik, Stanley M. and Kathleen Grey. 2005. "Stromatolites: Biogenicity, Biosignatures, and Bioconfusion." Astrobiology and Planetary Missions, Proceedings of the SPIE (Society of Photo-Optical Instrumentation Engineers) 5906: P1-P9. doi:10.1117/12.625556.

Kauffman, Erle G. and James R. Steidtmann. 1981. "Are these the Earliest Metazoan Trace Fossils?" *Journal of Paleontology* 55:923-947.

Knoll, Andrew H. 2003. *Life on a Young Planet: The First Three Billion Years of Evolution on Earth*. Princeton, New Jersey: Princeton University Press.

Schopf, J. William, ed. 1983. *Earth's Earliest Biosphere: Its Origin and Evolution*. Princeton, New Jersey: Princeton University Press.

Schopf, J. William. 1999. *Cradle of Life: The Discovery of Earth's Earliest Fossils*. Princeton, New Jersey: Princeton University Press.

Stinchcomb, Bruce L. 2007. *World's Oldest Fossils*. Atglen, Pennsylvania: Schiffer Publishing, Ltd.

Stinchcomb, Bruce L. 2011. *Jewels of the Early Earth: Minerals and Fossils of the Precambrian, 85–99*. Atglen, Pennsylvania: Schiffer Publishing Ltd.

Chapter Two

Stromatolites and the Earliest Fossil Evidence of Life

B. L. Stinchcomb

The 1859 publication of Charles Darwin's *On the Origin of Species* established clear evidence that life had evolved over geologic time. Fossils from what would become known as the Precambrian portion of geologic time were unknown in the mid-ninetheeth century—uncovering the Precambrian fossil record would be an involved and convoluted process that is still going on today and is entwined with the subject of this book. The Precambrian stromatolite story begins with fossils known as stromatoporoids. These curious layered structures are associated with fossil corals of

Paleozoic age (Hall 1852). Stromatoporoids were considered to be corals by early and mid-nineteenth-century paleontologists, but unlike stromatolites, there was never any doubt as to their being true fossils and hence having a biogenic origin. Stromatoporoids in the mid-nineteenth-century were known from Europe (both Wales and France), but were even better known from North America, where they were reported from eastern Ontario, Quebec, New York, Ohio, and Kentucky—especially at Falls of the Ohio near Louisville, Kentucky (Lesley 1890, LeConte 1910).

Figure 2-01. Stromatoporoid. Only recently (1989) were these fossils found to be a type of sponge. In the nineteenth century they were recognized as undoubted fossils, possibly of a primitive life form (corals); they never were considered not to be fossils. Their similarity to what, in the early twentieth entury, would be called stromatolites, was noted by many early twentieth century paleontologists—this similarity became the basis for some (but not all) paleontologists' consideration that stromatolites were biogenic. Note that this slice, though a stromatoporoid, resembles a fossil coral and that stromatoporoids are commonly associated with fossil corals. From the Middle Devonian, Callaway (Cedar Valley) Limestone, Fulton, Missouri.

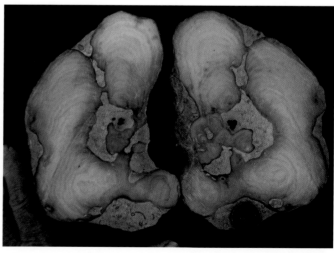

Figure 2-02. A sliced Devonian stromatoporoid showing minimal growth lines. Lithograph City Formation, Upper Devonian, Black Hawk County, Mesaerly, Iowa. *Specimen provided by Chris Cozart*

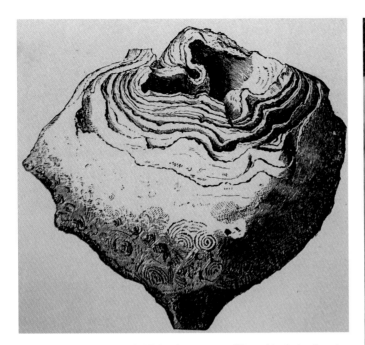

Figure 2-03. Illustrations of a typical Paleozoic stromatoporoid from a late nineteenth century work. Stromatoporoids were well known and recognized Paleozoic fossils by the mid nineteenth entury. Their relationship to what would be called stromatolites was puzzling, especially since stromatolites occurred in rocks much older than those containing stromatoporoids.

Figure 2-05. *Cryptozoon proliferium*, Hall, 1885. This was the first stromatolite to be formally recognized in paleontology and given a Linnean (scientific) name. Upper Cambrian, Saratoga, New York.

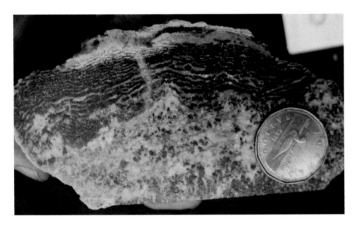

Figure 2-04. *Eozoön Canadense*, "the dawn animal of Canada," a misleading pseudofossil.

The next part of the stromatolite story was the discovery of *Eozoön Canadense* (the dawn animal of Canada) in the mid-1860s (Dawson 1865, Darwin 1872). Eozoön was discovered in very ancient (Precambrian) rocks of Quebec, as part of a search for fossils in these geologically ancient rocks. Such searches in Precambrian rocks began in earnest in the mid-nineteenth century looking for fossil ancestors of animals known in younger Cambrian rocks. As with the reef forming stromatoporoids, Eozoön occurs in what resemble reefs—but in this case they came from highly metamorphosed limestone, actually marble of the Precambrian Grenville Series of Quebec. As a fossil, Eozoön was considered to be a giant rhizopod or Foraminifera, a primitive single-celled "animal" that lived in primordial seas of what is now eastern Canada.

The next fossil in the stromatolite saga came from a fossil named Cryptozoon (Hall 1883). Occurring this time in Cambrian age rocks of upstate New York near the resort town of Saratoga, Cryptozoon, like Eozoön, was considered a giant rhizopod or Foraminifera. Unlike Eozoön, however, which turned out to be a pseudofossil, Cryptozoon was accepted by most geologists as an actual fossil.

Another significant "zoon" to turn up was Archeozoon, a fossil similar to Cryptozoon but coming from undoubted rocks of Precambrian age near St. Johns, New Brunswick, Canada. With the beginning of the twentieth century, more Cryptozoon-like structures had turned up; these were first given the moniker stromatolith in 1908 (Kalkowsky 1908), which, when anglicized, became stromatolite. Kalkowsky considered these structures to have formed from the life activities of a variety of "lower plants," which of course included algae. Noteworthy also in the complex history of stromatolites was Charles D. Walcott's 1914 paper, "Precambrian Algonkian Algal Flora," a work that described a variety of what were stromatolite-like objects from the Precambrian Belt Series of Montana and Idaho. Walcott was an astute fossil collector and an excellent field geologist. In the late nineteenth century he became head of the United States Geological Survey, and later, director of the

Smithsonian Institution. Today he is best known for the discovery of the Burgess Shale of British Columbia with its plethora of soft bodied, Cambrian-age animals marvelously preserved. These fossils were the basis of Stephen J. Gould's 1997 book, *Wonderful Life*.

Interest in stromatolites waned throughout the first half of the twentieth century, many geologists and paleontologists doubting their biogenic origin in part because they occurred in such ancient rocks. In the 1950s Elso S. Barghoorn, of Harvard University, published a paper with Stanley Tyler

Figure 2-06. *Archeozoon acadianese,* Matthew, 1890. The second stromatolite to be given a binomial Linnean name. Saint John, New Brunswick, Canada.

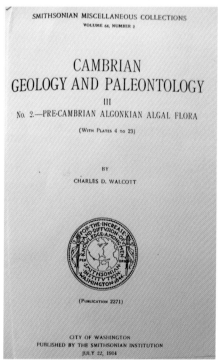

Figure 2-07. Title page of Walcott's *Precambrian Algonkian Algal Flora*, a seminal work on Precambrian stromatolites. Charles D. Walcott was a strong proponent for the biogenic origin of stromatolites.

Figure 2-8. Stephen J. Gould's book *Wonderful Life*. This informative and interesting work on the Cambrian Radiation Event is still in print.

Figure 2-09. *Stromatolite Newsletter.* A periodical publication started by French paleontologist Claude Monty in the late 1970s when interest in "stroms" developed within the paleontological community.

describing microfossils preserved in black chert of the Precambrian Gunflint Formation of Ontario (Tyler and Barghoorn 1954). These microfossils were considered to be various types of flagellated protozoans, blue-green algae, and fungi mostly associated with stromatolites. Geologic relationships and radiometric age dating had nailed down the age of the Gunflint Formation at about two billion years, and the fossils, preserved in very fine-grained flint or chert, were convincing.

A later paper (Barghoorn and Tyler 1965) documented a greater range of microfossils in the Gunflint Formation and also noted the association of most of these with stromatolites, which are abundant in the Gunflint Formation. This was followed by additional convincing evidence of similar microfossils in iron formation of the Lake Superior Region (LaBerge 1967). These microfossils occurring in stromatolites of great antiquity convinced many geologists of the biogenicity of most stromatolites and the existence of primitive life preserved deep in the Precambrian rock record.

By the 1980s, most geologists had accepted the biogenicity of stromatolites and thus of life's great antiquity (Schopf 1983). By the end of the twentieth century, the existence of abundant life in the Precambrian became an accepted paradigm, and this, in turn, led to an increased amount of discovery and publishing on Precambrian fossils. Today specialized journals, such as *Precambrian Research* and even those dealing with exobiology, focus on the fossils and biogenic record of the first three-and-a-half billion years of Earth's history.

The second decade of the twenty-first century has shown increased interest in communities of fossil microbes and the possibility that they may have once lived on Mars—this in turn has also given additional impetus to discovery and study of earthly stromatolites. Stromatolites receive enough interest today that they now have become a geo-collectible—a fossil serious collectors used to regard with contempt as "just algae."

Figure 2-10. "Stringy" and irregularly-shaped masses of jaspellite (red) suggest that gelatinous blobs of oxygen-producing-microbes may have been responsible for this portion of MISS (Microbial Induced Sedimentary Structure). This example of "slime thru time" is preserved in tuff-bearing sediment of the mid Proterozoic (Mesoproterozoic) of Missouri.

Figure 2-11. More stringy and elongate shaped mass of what were (probably) slimy blobs of photosynthetic microbes.

Microbial Induced Sedimentary Structures (MISS)

Possibly even older than stromatolites and more pervasive in some ancient rocks are lithic signatures known as MISS (Microbially Induced Sedimentary Structures). More subtle than stromatolites, these were originally films, globs, or chips of moneran mats that covered the sea bottom or other surfaces and then were preserved by partial mineralization. Also seen in MISS are distinctive granular and stringy patterns (or signatures), which are also found in most fossilized stromatolites. In the strictest sense of the term, stromatolites can be considered a form of MISS. However, even though MISS and stromatolites feature microbial mats as their main construction element, there are two major differences. The first difference is that MISS is a surface feature and is two-dimensional, while stromatolites exhibit a third dimension of stacked layers. The second difference is that stromatolites form in environments rich in carbonate, and MISS occur in silica-rich and evaporitic environments. Stromatolites exhibit a wide variety of morphologic and taxonomic variation, whereas MISS does not appear to have changed at all in morphology since its first appearance. Stromatolites could be considered a younger relative of MISS.

MISS also show textures, some of which are shown here, frequently seen in iron formation, a phenomena that supports a biogenic origin for that unique sedimentary rock. This is especially significant as there is metamorphosed iron formation in some of the earth's oldest rocks—almost four billion years old, spanning almost a third of the time since the "Big Bang," some 13.8 billion years ago.

Figure 2-12. Modern stringy and slimy photosynthetic moneran mats at Waimangu Volcanic Valley, New Zealand. These mats were probably similar to what made up MISS in the Proterozoic.

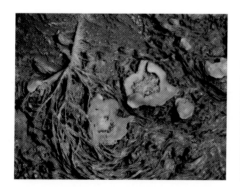

Figure 2-13. Close-up of slimy, gelatinous photosynthetic moneran mats illustrating the connection to MISS, Yellowstone National Park, Wyoming.

Figure 2-14. Red and gray stromatolite-like fragment of MISS (Microbially Induced Sedimentary Structures) surrounded by smaller masses of MISS. Stromatolites and MISS often exhibit the same textures; stromatolites can be considered as a specific and distinctive form of MISS.

Figure 2-15. Concentrations of small granules in this red MISS (Microbially Induced Sedimentary Structure) are found in both stromatolites and in iron formation, since they apparently had a common origin. These spherical granules are believed to have formed from the microfossil *Eospheria tyleri*, an organism that was probably a major component in the production of iron formation, according to LaBerge, 1967.

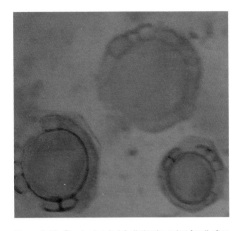

Figure 2-16. *Eospheria tyleri.* A distinctive microfossil often associated with iron formation and found in both stromatolites and iron formation. Some geologists think *Eospheria* was responsible for the small granules found in iron formation stromatolites and in other microbially induced sedimentary structures associated with iron formation. *Eospheria* may also have been responsible for both silica and iron deposition in iron formation.

Figure 2-17. A clast showing stromatolite-like laminae that includes red jaspellite layers. The later may originate from microbes that produced generous amounts of free oxygen. *Eospheria tyleri* may have been responsible for this.

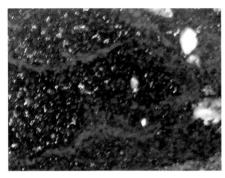

Figure 2-18. Granular red masses of jaspellite, which some geologists believe originated with a nucleus of *Eospheria*. Such occurrences are common in Early Proterozoic and Archean Iron Formation.

"Stroms" and the First Animal Life

Stromatolites represent a moneran-based ecosystem that goes back over three billion years. Starting in the Cambrian Period, "stroms" are frequently associated with a variety of animal fossils (or better, one might say that many early animal fossils appear to be associated with "stroms"). Older than 530 million years, stromatolites lack any associated animal fossils; these older occurrences consist only of the "stroms" themselves, with nothing else of obvious biogenic origin (oncolites and Edicarian organisms excepted). This is most readily explained by the fact that animals were not around—they had not yet evolved! If higher life forms were around, they probably were not yet associated with "stroms" and also may have been soft bodied so that it was difficult for them to leave a fossil record. This is the view taken prior to the 1960s when the moneran-stromatolite-ecosystem concept was introduced. Starting with the Cambrian Period (beginning some 530 million years ago, depending upon who does the radiometric age dating), "stroms" can be found associated with a variety of invertebrates, usually invertebrate animals like monoplacophorans, gastropods, and trilobites (Stitt 1976). This stromatolite-dominated ecosystem appears to have been a very successful one until the middle part of the Ordovician Period when invertebrate life diversified to the point where it cropped the "stroms" to such an extent that they now only could live in hypersaline or other environments where animal life was excluded. Stromatolite-dominated ecosystems that included invertebrates were thus

Figure 2-19. Ediacaran Vendozoans. These puzzling fossils from the late Neoproterozoic are found in strata underlying that of Cambrian age. They may represent some sort of evolutionary "experiment" in the late Precambrian consisting of eukaryotic cells incorporated into a moneran mat. Late Precambrian bedding surfaces also sometimes show what is believed to be impressions of extensive moneran mats that formed on the floor of a seaway. Mistaken Point fossil preserve, eastern Newfoundland.

Figure 2-20. Archaeocyathids. These puzzling reef-forming organisms flourished for a million years or so during the latter part of the Lower Cambrian. They formed reefs in environments where stromatolites are normally found, except when archaeocyathids are present. This suggests that Archaeocyathids usurped or commandeered environments that otherwise would have been occupied by stromatolites.

Figure 2-21. Bruce Stinchcomb at a silicified mass of Cambrian digitate stromatolites in the northeastern Ozarks of Missouri. Stromatolite reefs in the late Cambrian became a common and luxurious marine environment that harbored a variety of mollusks. This stromatolite-dominated ecosystem was especially prevalent in the Late Cambrian and Early Ordovician.

especially characteristic of the Cambrian and the early portion of the Ordovician Period (the Lower Ordovician).

The Last of Widespread Stromatolite-Dominated Ecosystems

The dominant and obvious evidence for life in the Precambrian is the ubiquitous presence of stromatolites! However, "stroms," which grew in shallow-water marine environments, are widespread fossils in Cambrian age strata as well. Stromatolites flourished in the Cambrian just as much as they did in the Precambrian. The Lower Cambrian presents a noticeable absence of stromatolites, especially when the puzzling archeocyathids are prevalent. It appears that the reef-forming archeocyathids took the place of stromatolites during this time, but with extinction of the archeocyathids at the end of the Lower Cambrian, stromatolite reefs returned. After the early part of the Ordovician Period, the Lower Ordovician, stromatolites

Figure 2-22. These clusters of sponges were found at the location in the previous figure. Sponges such as these are intimately associated with digitate stromatolites and are part of a Cambrian stromatolite-dominated ecosystem.

Figure 2-23. Cambrian and Lower Ordovician stromatolite-dominated animal associations are well represented in fossils found over the Ozark Uplift of southern Missouri and northern Arkansas. Often these are found as chert "cores," which are silicified masses containing fossil mollusks that lived in association with stromatolites. The animals, which presumably fed on the stromatolites, are arranged in distinctive positions that show where they lived inside or near the stromatolites. This group of monoplacophorans lived in digitate stromatolites and left elongated holes large enough to insert a finger.

Figure 2-24. A group of tergomyans that lived inside cavities formed by a group of globular stromatolites.

Figure 2-25. A Cambrian snail-like mollusk (*Scaevogyra*) associated with digitate stromatolites, which are denoted by pens inserted where the stromatolite "fingers" existed. *Scaevogyra* is often associated with the *Hypseloconus* sp. (a monoplacophoran), both of which were part of a Cambrian stromatolite-dominated-ecosystem.

Figure 2-26. Early cephalopods. These early representatives of the octopus and squid lived in association with stromatolite reefs where, like their monoplacophoran ancestors, they likely fed on stromatolites. These cephalopods, some of the oldest known, come from strata of latest Cambrian (or earliest Ordovician) age in the Missouri Ozarks.

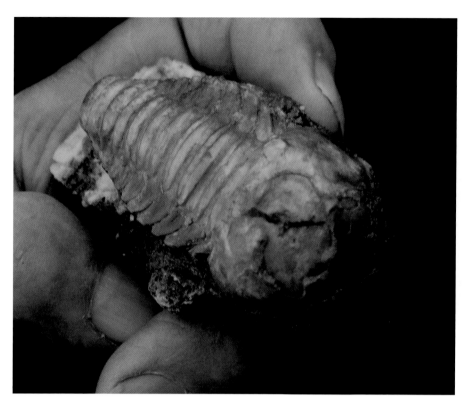

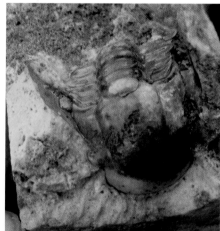

Figure 2-27. Trilobite of the genus *Stenopilus*. This trilobite is always found associated with stromatolites. Unlike most other Cambrian trilobites, *Stenopilus* lived among stromatolite reefs in a stromatolite-dominated-ecosystem (Stitt 1976).

Figure 2-28. *Plethopeltis* sp. This trilobite, like *Stenopilus* lived in association with stromatolites in seas of the latest Cambrian of Laurentian North America.

again become much less common and by the end of the Ordovician they had all but disappeared.

If you had a time machine and could program it to go back into that vast time span that constitutes the Precambrian, stromatolites would be the most dominant evidence of life. If, however, you then programmed your time machine to go into the Cambrian Period, a whole "new" and different world of life would appear, but stromatolites would still abound. They would form widespread reefs in the shallow water with about the same frequency as they did in the Precambrian, but they would now share this water with numerous animals and plants.

Cambrian Animals and Stromatolites

In the deeper waters of the Cambrian seas would be found trilobites and trilobite-like animals, many of them soft-bodied. These soft-bodied organisms would include the weird animals of the Burgess shale and Cheng Chang faunas. The Burgess is covered in Stephen J. Gould's book *Wonderful Life*. In making this Cambrian leap through time, you would have crossed the Precambrian-Cambrian boundary and entered the weird world of the Cambrian radiation event. Now living intimately among stromatolites in a stromatolite-dominated ecosystem would be a variety of animals which, for the first time, would bear shells. Included would be the strange monoplacophorans and tergomyans and various types of multi-plated mollusks, along with gastropods (snails) and rostrochonchs. The

puzzling hyoliths might also be present, along with other types of mollusk-like animals, some with snail-like shells. Many of these animals, like other Cambrian organisms, had body plans spun off of animal-life's early template, and many would become extinct near the Cambrian Period's end, some 500 million years ago.

Lower Ordovician Animals and a Stromatolite-Dominated Ecosystem

The shallow water stromatolite-dominated ecosystem of the Cambrian Period continued into the early part of the Ordovician Period (the Lower Ordovician). Here, besides some of the weird-shelled animals like those of the Cambrian, would be found various types of shelled cephalopods. All of these animals were intimately associated with stromatolites, upon which they almost certainly fed. This intimate stromatolite-animal association ended with the end of the Lower Ordovician and the appearance of various "new" body plans. This also marks the beginning of the Middle Ordovician, a time when these "new" types of invertebrate body plans spread over the globe and stromatolites became rare. This time of stromatolite reduction and corresponding introduction of new animal body-plans is known as GODE (the Great Ordovician Diversification Event). Thus begins a "new" chapter in the history of life.

Figure 2-29. A group of Lower Ordovician gastropods (snails), which were associated with extensive stromatolite reefs. These occur in a "core" or chert-filled cavity that formed between the stromatolites. Gasconade Formation, Lower Ordovician, Missouri Ozarks.

Figure 2-30. *Sinuopea regalis*. A pair of these large gastropods preserved in a "core" that formed between a group of stromatolites. Gasconade Formation, Crawford County, Missouri.

Figure 2-31. *Helicotoma ungulata*. These gastropods often occur in pairs like this where they lived in a cavity between stromatolites. It has been suggested that these pairs represent male and female individuals living in "bliss" between "stroms," which presumably provided their food.

Figure 2-32. Primitive cephalopods (ellesmeroids). These early ancestors of the octopus and squid, like their monoplacophoran ancestors, lived between stromatolites in extensive reefs. Like the gastropods, these are usually associated with "cores" formed in the center of a group of stromatolites.

Glossary

Biogenic. Being, or once having been, a part of the biosphere. Many Precambrian phenomena, especially stromatolites, have been questioned at various times as to their biogenic origin. Determining if some geologically ancient structure or object was or was not of biogenic origin can be difficult and often muddy—such was the case with stromatolites until the 1960s.

Edicarian organisms. Organisms responsible for puzzling fossils found in very late Precambrian rock, not considered animals by the author and other paleontologists.

Exobiology. A branch of biology concerned with the search for life outside the earth and with the effects of extraterrestrial environments on living organisms—also called astrobiology.

Foraminifera. A group (order) of usually small "shelled," single-celled organisms belonging to the Kingdom Protista. In the nineteenth century, Foraminifera were known as Rhizopods, and Eozoön Canadense was considered as such.

Grenville Series. A thick sequence of metamorphosed strata of mid-Precambrian age, which includes thick beds of marble. Rocks of the Grenville Series crop out in eastern Ontario, western Quebec, in New York's Adirondack Mountains, and in western New Jersey, where the Grenville Marble is the host rock to the many fluorescent minerals of the Franklin and Sterling Hill Mines.

Hyolith. An extinct animal with a tapered shell. Hyoliths have been classified as mollusks and are placed in their own extinct phylum. They are especially characteristic of the Cambrian Period, but range through the entire Paleozoic Era.

Protozoans. Single-celled organisms made up of protoplasm much like that of an amoeba, but housed in a perforated, calcareous "shell" (or test) from which protoplasm streams. Protozoa are known today as the Kingdom Protista; Foraminifera and amoeba both belong to this kingdom.

Bibliography

Awramik, Stanley M. 2006. "Respect for Stromatolites." *Nature*, 441:700-701.

Barghoorn, Elso S. and Stanley A. Tyler. 1965. "Microorganisms from the Gunflint Chert." *Science*, 147:563-575. doi:10.1126/science.147.3658.563.

Darwin, Charles. 1872. "Chapter 9: On the Imperfection of the Geologic Record." In *On the Origin of Species by Means of Natural Selection*, 7th Ed. London: John Murray.

Dawson, John W. 1865. "On Certain Organic Remains in the Laurentian Limestones of Canada." One of the papers presented on the history of Eozoön Canadense. The Canadian Naturalist, 2:99-111.

Gould, Stephen J. 1990. *Wonderful Life: The Burgess Shale and the Nature of History*. New York: W.W. Norton.

Hagadorn, James W., Friedrich Pflüger, and David J. Bottjer, eds. 1999. "Unexplored microbial worlds." *Palaios*, 14:1-93.

Hall, James. 1852. *Paleontology of New York, Vol. 2*, "Organic Remains of the Lower Middle Division of the New-York System." New York State Geological Survey, Albany, New York.

Hall, James. 1883. Plate VI and explanation: Cryptozoon, n. g.; Cryptozoon proliferum n. sp. In *Thirty-sixth Annual Report on the New York State Museum of Natural History to the Legislature*, edited by H. R. Pierson, New York Senate paper 1883/53, Albany, New York.

Kalkowsky, Ernst. 1908. "Oolith und stromatolith im norddeutschen Buntsandstein," *Zeitschrift der Deutschen Geologischen Gesellschaft*. 60:68-125.

LaBerge, Gene L. 1967. "Microfossils and Precambrian Iron-Formations." *Geological Society of America Bulletin*, 78:331-342.

Lesley, J. Peter. 1890. *A Dictionary of the Fossils of Pennsylvania and Neighboring States named in the Reports and Catalogues of the Survey, Vol. 3*. Pennsylvania Geological Survey, Harrisburg Pennsylvania.

LeConte, Joseph. 1910. *Elements of Geology*. New York: D. Appleton.

Noffke, Nora, Alan W. Decho, and Paul Stoodle. 2013. "Slime through time: The fossil record of prokaryote evolution," *Palaios*, 28:1-5.

Schopf, J. William, ed. 1983. *Earth's Earliest Biosphere: Its Origin and Evolution*. Princeton, NJ: Princeton University Press.

Stinchcomb, Bruce L. and Nicholas A. Angeli. 2002. "New Cambrian and Lower Ordovician Monoplacophorans from the Ozark Uplift, Missouri." *Journal of Paleontology*, 76:965-974.

Stitt, James H. 1976. "Functional morphology and the life habits of the late Cambrian trilobite *Stenopilus pronus* Raymond." *Journal of Paleontology*, 50:561-576.

Tyler, Stanley A. and Elso S. Barghoorn. 1954. "Occurrence of Structurally Preserved Plants in Pre-Cambrian Rocks of the Canadian Shield." *Science*, 119: 606-608.

Walcott, Charles D. 1914. "Cambrian geology and paleontology, III: Pre-Cambrian Algonkian algal flora." Smithsonian Miscellaneous Collections, 64:77-156.

Walter, Malcolm R., ed. 1976. *Stromatolites* (Developments in Sedimentology, Vol. 20) Elsevier Scientific, Amsterdam.

Chapter Three

Significance of Stromatolites to Atmospheric Oxygen and Banded Iron Formations

R. J. Leis

Another amazing fact I found out about stromatolites once I began to study them was how they helped to oxygenate the atmosphere. Before stromatolites or photosynthetic monerans existed, the atmosphere was virtually devoid of free oxygen (O_2).

How do we know that primitive early photosynthetic bacteria provided oxygen to the atmosphere? The answer to this can be found in Banded Iron Formation (BIF).

First what is BIF? Although this material is not a stromatolite, it can be layered like one and can also be the result of stromatolitic activity, and can exhibit MISS. BIF can also be considered in some ways as a chemical trace fossil. Typical BIF will consist of repeated layers of iron oxides (either magnetite or hematite) alternating with thin layers (millimeter to centimeters in thickness) of red, yellow, or cream-colored layers of chert (silica) or jasper. BIF generally has more than 15 percent iron content.

Some BIF dates as old as 3.8 b.y.a. (Isua Series of Greenland) but most are aged at around 2.5 billion to 1.8 b.y.a., most occurring in the Proterozoic era. Isua BIF is the oldest sedimentary rock in the world and is from the Isua Supercrustal Belt in southwestern Greenland. Some geologists have concluded that the carbon isotopic composition of graphite found in some of the Isua BIF is consistent with a biogenic origin. The dark layers are rich in iron oxide and the lighter layers contain varying amounts of the mineral graphite. Some Isua researchers believe that the graphite in these rocks is inorganic in origin and formed by various metamorphic chemical reactions.

Figure 3-1. Isua BIF clearly showing distinct layering even after severe metamorphism. *Photo courtesy of Spencer G. Lucas, New Mexico Museum of Natural History and Science, Albuquerque, New Mexico*

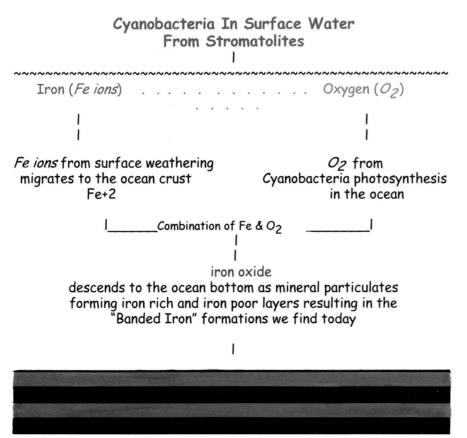

Figure 3-2. An illustrated example of the process by which oxygen produced by cyanobacteria combines with iron ions in the ocean to form BIF.

Compared to other geological deposits, the BIFs are controversial regarding the mechanism by which they were formed. The method of formation presented here is probably the most widely accepted explanation at present. It is believed that solutions of components of the ocean crust, and weathering of newly formed continental rocks, led to a high level of iron entering the oceans in the form of soluble iron ions (ferrous iron, Fe^{2+}). At the same time, stromatolites formed and perhaps other primitive photosynthetic organisms may have become abundant. Monerans, which were responsible for stromatolites, produced free oxygen (O_2) as a by-product of photosynthesis.

This oxygen combined with the water-soluble ferrous iron ions to form magnetite, hematite, or iron oxide (both non-soluble ferric iron, Fe^{3+}), which sank to the sea floor, forming iron rich layers. This process was cyclical and resulted in iron-rich layers, dark in color, of hematite or magnetite and relatively iron-poor layers often red in color. Another hypothesis of BIF formation involves anoxygenic photoautotrophic bacteria living beneath the ocean's surface-mixing-layer and speculates that these organisms may have precipitated the free iron being released by black smokers (hydrothermal vents) into iron oxide. See the bibliography (Kappler 2005) for an article on this hypothesis.

Figure 3-3. An illustration to help visualize the cyclical nature of how BIF was formed.

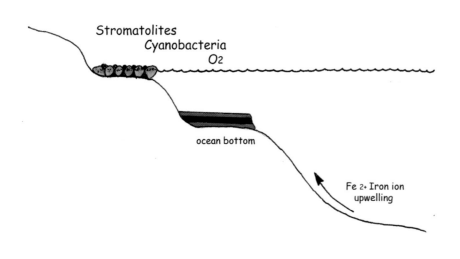

There are also several hypotheses about the cyclical nature of BIF. One hypothesis is that it formed from upwelling currents that were perhaps seasonal and would bring soluble ferrous iron ions up to the oxygenated parts of the ocean, where they then would become insoluble ferric iron oxide-forming BIF. Another explanation is "bacterial suicide." Primitive photosynthetic bacteria could not tolerate oxygen. The early oxygen produced by cyanobacteria was almost completely used up when it came into contact with iron ions in the ocean and formed iron oxide. This cleansed the bacteria's environment. As the cyanobacteria and bacteria expanded beyond the capacity for the iron in the oceans to neutralize the waste O_2, the oxygen content of the oceans rose to toxic levels. This increase in oxygen resulted in large-scale die-off of the photosynthesizers and led to accumulations of iron-poor chert layers on the sea floor. In time, the photosynthetic bacteria would once again build up and a new iron-rich chert layer would begin to accumulate. No matter what caused the cycles and abrupt layers, there never seemed to be a time when the iron-rich layer or the iron-poor chert formations produced layers thicker than approximately four inches.

At approximately 1.8 billion years ago, abundant BIF ceased to form. At this point, most of the available iron ions had combined with oxygen to form iron oxide and had become BIF. Since there were no more iron ions to combine with oxygen, the atmosphere began to increase its oxygen content. Stromatolites had evolved at this point so they could now exist in this oxygenated atmosphere. It was also about this time that some multi-celled organisms may have appeared (*Grypania* sp).

There are two major types of iron formation—Algoma-type and Superior-type. Algoma-type is usually Archean in age and more localized. Superior-type iron formation is usually associated with the Mid-Precambrian. It is well layered and sometimes found with stromatolites, illustrating its biogenic origins more so than with the Algoma-type. In contrast to Algoma-type iron formations, the Superior-type BIF generally extends over large areas.

When it comes to the production of iron ore, BIF is king! BIF makes up many meters of rock and contains by far the greatest deposits of iron ore on the planet. BIF are found on every continent's continental shields. Once you locate them you will find iron ore sources to mine. Most of the world's steel industries are based on iron ores laid down by monerans billions of years ago. Whenever you drive your car or use a product made of steel you can reflect on how this ultimately was made possible by Precambrian photosynthetic bacteria and cyanobacteria.

BIF is collectible and in many instances can be quite beautiful, especially when polished. Most BIF has been metamorphosed to some degree and often has also undergone faulting, fracturing, folding, and compaction.

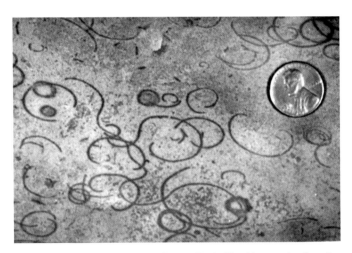

Figure 3-4. Slab of *Grypania* sp. spirals from the Empire Mine, Negaunee Iron-formation, near Negaunee, Michigan. This is a photo of a fossilized 1.88 b.y.a. eukaryotic celled organism and is some of the earliest evidence of multicelled life going back into the Precambrian. *Provided by Tsu-Ming Han through the courtesy of Gene LaBerge*

Figure 3-5. Major Precambrian iron-bearing shields of the earth.

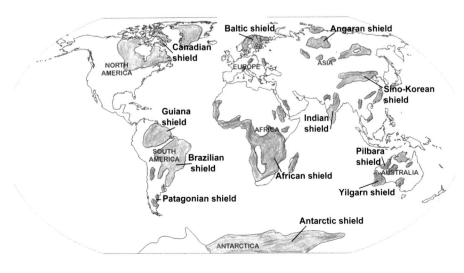

Figure 3-6. An Algoma-type BIF approximately seven miles south of Wawa, Ontario, Canada, along Highway 17. It is Archean in age. The stromatolite-like layering is clearly evident. This BIF does not have the red, yellow, or cream-colored layers typical of Superior-type BIF.

Figure 3-7. Abandoned and water-filled Macleod Mine, Wawa, Ontario, Canada. The iron from the BIF along Highway 17, just south of Wawa, is different from that found in this mine. The iron from both sites is similar in age, but the roadside iron formation contains minerals made of oxides of iron. The minerals in the abandoned Macleod Mine are made of carbonates of iron. The minerals from the roadside cut will attract a magnet; those in the iron ore mine will not.

Figure 3-8. Another photo of the Algoma-type BIF, Wawa, Ontario, Canada. This site overlies volcanic rocks, which is typical of Algoma-type BIF.

Figure 3-9. Surface view of the Algoma-type BIF, Wawa, Ontario, Canada. This BIF formation covers a localized area, another trait of Algoma-type BIF.

Figure 3-10. Slab of Algoma-type BIF, Soudan Iron Formation, St. Louis County, Minnesota, approximately 2.7 b.y.a., Archean age. *Photo courtesy of Gene LaBerge*

Figure 3-11. Slab of Algoma-type BIF, Soudan Iron Formation, St. Louis County, Minnesota, approximately 2.7 b.y.a. Note how iron and non-iron are not evenly layered.

Figure 3-12. Slab of Algoma-type BIF from the (2.8 b.y.) Goldman Meadows Formation, South Pass Greenstone Belt, South Pass Iron Mine, South Pass, Wyoming.

Figure 3-13. Block of Algoma-type BIF from the Soudan Iron Formation, St. Louis County, Minnesota, approximately 2.7 b.y.a. Again note the non-layered look.

Figure 3-14. An Archean banded iron specimen sculpted by the winds into a banded iron ventifact from the Kalahari Desert, South Africa.

Figure 3-15. Superior-type BIF from Mt. Whittlesey, Mellen, Wisconsin. This type of formation is also sometimes referred to as even-bedded, approximately 1.8–1.9 b.y.a.

Figure 3-16. Another photo of Superior-type BIF from just east of Mellen, Wisconsin; again note the even layering. This particular iron formation covers a large area, which is a trait of Superior-type BIF.

Figure 3-17. Another characteristic of Superior-type BIF is that it is commonly associated with stromatolites such as the Oncolitic stromatolites found near the BIF east of Mellen, Wisconsin, which are approximately 1.8–1.9 b.y.a. *Photo courtesy of Gene LaBerge*

Figure 3-19. A glacial Superior-type BIF nugget found near Ishpeming, Michigan; this specimen is the size of a basketball and weighs about 300 pounds. Note the even layering in this type of BIF.

Figure 3-18. A formation of Superior-type BIF, sometimes referred to as "Jaspellite," consists of rock composed of alternating layers of red jasper (a variety of quartz) and hematite. This specimen is from the New York Mine, Ishpeming, Michigan, and is approximately 1.8 b.y. old.

Figure 3-20. Beautiful slab of Superior-type BIF from the Nagaunee Iron Formation, Incline Mine, Ishpeming, Michigan, approximately 1.8 b.y.a. The relatively even red chert layers are clearly visible.

Figure 3-21. Large slab of snakeskin jasper from Turee Creek Station about 100 miles southwest of Newman in the Pilbara Region of Western Australia. This material occurs as seams of jaspellite in a banded iron formation called "The Weeli Wooli Formation" and is approximately 2.5 b.y.a. Some experts think this is a form of BIF; others think it might be stromatolitic.

Figure 3-23. Fragment of Tiger iron, Archean, 2.73 b.y.a., South Africa, Africa.

Figure 3-24. Highly metamorphosed BIF known as Marramamba Tiger eye, Archean, Port Hedland, Western Australia.

Figure 3-22. Polished slab of BIF known as Tiger iron. The yellow bands are Tiger eye (also called Tiger's eye), the red is jasper, and the bluish bands are hematite; from the Hamersley iron district of Western Australia, Archean in age.

Figure 3-25. A beautiful piece of BIF from the Hopkins Mine, Cuyuna Range, Minnesota, 2–2.2 b.y.a. Geologists theorize that a geothermal vent injected rhodochrosite/rhodonite into the already existing BIF.

Figure 3-26. A slab of botryoidal hematite that appears to have been injected with rhodochrosite. This material is also known as "kidney ore" and is from Tieta Iroud, Morocco, North Africa, Precambrian in age.

Figure 3-27. Our North American equivalent to the Tiger eye of Australia and Africa is Binghamite and silkstone, which are rockhound terms. This North American Tiger eye is less common than the Australian and African types. This slab, like all Binghamite/silkstone, is from the Cuyuna Iron Range, Crow Wing County, Minnesota, and is approximately 2 b.y.a. A man named Bill Bingham discovered this material on mine dumps in 1936 and found the material to be excellent for lapidary purposes. This is a rare and unusual form of BIF.

Figure 3-29. Gem-quality Binghamite is usually red or yellow, exhibiting a chatoyant luster similar to Australian or African Tiger's eye.

Figure 3-28. Binghamite is composed of filamentous quartz that forms in all directions with inclusions of goethite or hematite.

Figure 3-30. A block of material exhibiting silkstone. Silkstone is similar to Binghamite, but its quartz crystals are arranged in a level line and the stone is more opaque and coarsely fibrous than Binghamite. Silkstone is often brown but can be yellow, grayish green, blue gray, or a combination of these colors. It has a marked and wavy chatoyancy and is commonly associated with asbestos. While not as highly prized by lapidarists, it is another beautiful and interesting form of BIF.

Figure 3-31. Iron ore stromatolite from the Pilbara Region of Western Australia 2.7 b.y.a. During the time of BIF, iron oxides in the oceans combined with oxygen to produce the world's iron ranges. Some of the iron oxides that were being produced were incorporated into the growing stromatolites at this time to produce the iron rich stromatolite you see in this specimen at the museum at Shark Bay.

Figure 3-32. A chunk of Mary Ellen Jasper, *Collenia undosa*, Biwabik Iron Formation, St. Louis County, Minnesota, 1.8–1.9 b.y.a. This specimen exhibits secondary iron formation. Hematite from groundwater has replaced the carbonate of the stromatolite.

Glossary

Botryoidal. Shaped like a bunch of grapes; especially used in describing mineral formations such as botryoidal hematite.

Carbonate. A descriptive term used for rocks and other earth materials that have an abundance of calcium carbonate ($CaCO_3$).

Chatoyant. Having a changeable luster or color with an undulating narrow band of white light (cat's-eye effect).

Chert. As a mineral: cryptocrystalline variety of quartz; as a rock: compact siliceous rock of varying color sometimes composed of microorganisms or precipitated silica grains.

Eukaryote. Any organism whose cells contain a nucleus and other organelle structures enclosed within membranes, one of the three domains of life

Ferrous Iron. Iron that has lost two electrons and therefore is in a more reduced state than ferric iron; ferrous iron compounds are usually water-soluble

Goethite. A mineral, iron oxyhydroxide FeO(OH), occurring in yellow or brown earthy masses and in crystals; a common ore of iron.

Hematite. An iron oxide mineral with iron in the ferric state..

Iron oxide. Chemical compounds composed of iron and oxygen, such as ferric oxide or ferrous oxide.

Jasper. Red to brown cryptocrystalline chemically precipitated quartz.

Magnetite. A strongly magnetic iron oxide mineral.

Metamorphism. Recrystallization of an existing rock; typically occurs at high temperatures and high pressure.

Monerans. Any organism of the taxonomic kingdom Monera, single-celled organisms that reproduce by splitting in two (binary fission) and have no cell nucleus; a kingdom of life in which all members are prokaryotes.

Photosynthesis. A metabolic process carried out by photosynthetic bacteria, cyanobacteria, algae, and plants in which light energy is converted to chemical energy and stored in molecules of carbohydrates; oxygen is released as a waste product of this process.

Rhodochrosite. A rose-red mineral consisting essentially of manganese carbonate.

Rhodonite. A pink to rose-red mineral, essentially a glassy crystalline manganese silicate.

Silica. A hard, unreactive, colorless compound that occurs as the mineral quartz and as a principal constituent of sandstone and other rocks.

Siliceous. A rock or plant containing silica.

Ventifact. A rock that has been shaped, polished, or faceted by wind-driven sand.

Bibliography

Bekker, Andrey, H.D. Holland, P.-L. Wang, D. Rumble III, H.J. Stein, J.L. Hannah, L.L. Coetzee and N.J. Beukes. 2004. "Dating the rise of atmospheric oxygen." *Nature*, 427:117-120. doi:10.1038/nature02260.

Chi Fru, Ernest, Magnus Ivarsson, Stephanos P. Kilias, Stefan Bengtson, Veneta Belivanova, Federica Marone, Danielle Fortin, Curt Broman and Marco Stampanoni. 2013. "Fossilized iron bacteria reveal a pathway to the biological origin of banded iron formation." *Nature Communications*, 4, number: 2050. doi:10.1038/ncomms3050

Gole, Martin J. and Cornelis Klein. 1981. "Banded iron-formations through much of Precambrian time." *Journal of Geology*, 89:169-183.

Harnmeijer, Jelte P. 2003. *Banded Iron Formation: A Continuing Enigma of Geology*. University of Washington Doc, p.1-25.

Kappler, Andreas, Claudia Pasquero, Kurt O. Konhauser, and Dianne K. Newman. 2005. "Deposition of banded iron formations by anoxygenic phototrophic Fe(II)-oxidizing bacteria." *Geology* 33:865-868.

Konhauser, Kurt O., Tristan Hamade, Rob Raiswell, Richard C. Morris, F. Grant Ferris, Gordon Southam, and Donald E. Canfield. 2002. "Could bacteria have formed the Precambrian banded iron formations?" *Geology*, 30:1079-1082.

Klein, Cornelis. 2005. "Some Precambrian banded iron-formations (BIFs) from around the world: Their age, geologic setting, mineralogy, metamorphism, geochemistry and origins." *American Mineralogist*, 90:1473-1499.

LaBerge, Gene L. 1994. *Geology of the Lake Superior Region*. Tucson, AZ: Geoscience Press.

Schopf, J. William. 2006. "Fossil evidence of Archaean life." *Philosophical Transactions of the Royal Society*, 361:869-885.

Chapter Four

Archean Stromatolites

B. L. Stinchcomb

Archean Rocks and Outcrops—Their Stromatolites

Probably the most intriguing aspect of stromatolites is their great geologic age! They are found in some of the earth's most ancient strata, laid down in what is known as the Archean Era of geologic time. Since the oldest Archean strata is almost four billion years old, that is some 85 percent of the age of the earth itself. Stromatolites in Archean rocks are rare, but probably not because life was a rare and localized phenomena on the earth at that time, as some have stated. Rather, it's probably safe to say that microbial life was commonplace on the early Earth, and the rarity of its evidence in these ancient rocks was a consequence of the following:

Shallow water, continental shelf environments (where stromatolites thrive) were locally quite limited during the Archean because there was a minimum of continental crust. This limited the amount of shallow water within the photic zone where photosynthesis and sea-bottom attachment could take place.

Little of the early earthly rock record has been preserved, since much of it has been destroyed by erosion, subduction, and metamorphism.

Archean strata that might contain stromatolites is rare. These ancient rocks have to be buried deep in the

Figure 4-1. Artist's interpretation of an Archean landscape. The oxygen-free atmosphere of the early Earth is believed to have been red in color; the moon's orbit was closer to the earth, so it would have appeared much larger in the sky. Stromatolites in the Archean occupied limited continental shelf areas, as the continents were just beginning to form.

Figure 4-2. Typical Archean outcrop I. Archean rocks had to be deeply buried to be preserved from erosion for billions of years. This deep burial made the rock quite hard and resistant to erosion when it eventually was exposed at the earth's surface. This is a typical Archean outcrop; its blocky appearance is caused by fractures produced by deep burial.

Figure 4-3. Typical Archean outcrop II. Archean metagreywacke with severe contortion produced from deep burial in the crust and metamorphism. Mount Zirkel, Colorado.

Figure 4-4. Typical Archean outcrop III. Buried deep in the earth's crust, these ancient rocks have become "cooked" or metamorphosed. This is the most frequent condition of Archean rock, and being so highly changed (metamorphosed), these rocks rarely preserve fossils in any part of geologic time. Most Archean rocks are devoid of any type of direct evidence of life, with the possible exception of some containing graphite. Archean rocks are often shot full of veins and dikes like these in this outcrop in western Ontario.

Figure 4-5. Typical Archean outcrop IV. Black, metamorphosed sediments often characterize Archean rocks since little (or no) free oxygen was present in the atmosphere at this time—any free oxygen produced by photosynthesis was immediately removed. These chemically-reducing conditions resulted in black, carbon-rich sediments in which any iron present usually would be in the ferrous oxidization state.

crust to be preserved from erosion over long spans of time—a prerequisite which (compared to younger strata) is relatively uncommon.

Younger strata often cover Archean strata, which had to be removed during more recent geologic time. Much of the Archean record is still buried under younger rock strata.

Archean stromatolites and other biogenic phenomena in these ancient rocks is subtle and usually takes a persistent and trained eye to spot.

Archean stromatolites are often similar to those of the early Proterozoic (Paleoproterozoic), but many do exhibit some distinctions. These distinctions resulted, at least in part, from the earth's atmosphere most likely being composed of carbon dioxide, water vapor, and nitrogen, with little or no free oxygen—that is, they often formed in what is known as a chemically-reducing environment. Archean stromatolites reflect this fact in that many are of dark hued "colors" (grays and/or black) reflecting these reducing conditions. This might be expected as the Archean atmosphere was also a reducing one which may, in the early Archean, have even contained methane, a strong chemical-reducing agent.

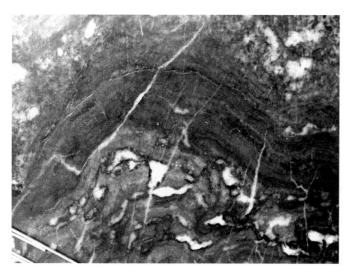

Figure 4-6. Archean stromatolites are often black or dark gray because many of them formed under reducing conditions where there was an absence of free oxygen.

Figure 4-7. Chunk of Archean iron formation (BIF), which is often massive and lacks any clear biogenic structures like stromatolites. A number of "signatures" are characteristic of Archean iron formation, which is believed to have been deposited in deep water of the earth's primordial ocean. This type of BIF is known as Algoma-type iron formation and shows what are known as MISS (Microbially Induced Sedimentary Structures).

Archean Iron Formation

Iron-formation or banded iron-formation (BIF) is a unique and distinctive sedimentary rock of frequent occurrence in some Archean strata. It is believed to have been formed from the oxidization of ferrous iron to ferric by free oxygen generated locally through photosynthesis. Characteristic beds of Archean iron-formation consist of thick, massive beds of alternating jasper, hematite, and quartz—a type of iron formation known as Algoma-type. This is in contrast with iron formation of the Proterozoic, which generally is more stratified and may even contain digitate stromatolites. Much Archean and Early Proterozoic iron formation, if not too metamorphosed, is made of small blobs and spherical granules. These are believed to be biogenic in origin—a product of co-precipitation of hematite and silica assisted by photosynthetic microbes (LaBerge 1967), some of which are shown in Figure 4-10. These granules can form as major components of previously mentioned MISS (Microbially Induced Sedimentary Structures).

Younger Proterozoic iron formation (Superior-type) appears to have been deposited in relatively shallow water that covered continental crust, an entity of rare occurrence in the Archean. Algoma-type iron formation, by contrast, is believed to have been deposited in the deeper water of the open ocean. This would agree with the Archean model of an earth with little continental crust, the planet at the time being mostly covered by a universal ocean. Because banded iron formation can contain stromatolites and be an attractive rock, it is widely used as a semi-precious stone (jasper or jaspellite).

Figure 4-8. Bedded (or layered) but still massive Archean iron formation of the Algoma-type is shown in this cut in the 2.7 b.y. old Soudan Iron Formation of northern Minnesota.

Figure 4-9. Younger (Paleoproterozoic) iron formation known as Superior-type iron formation is mined in northern Minnesota. Superior-type iron formation is often well-layered and may contain obvious stromatolites.

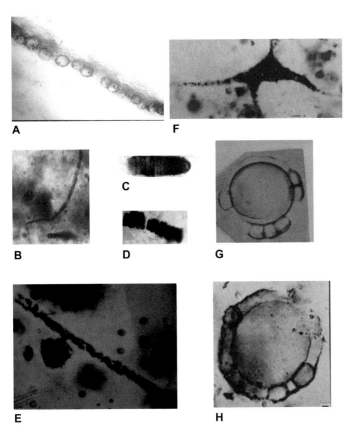

Figure 4-10. Microfossils from stromatolite-bearing beds of the Early Proterozoic Gunflint Chert. These are associated with stromatolites from the Biwabik Iron Formation or with the Gunflint Chert of adjacent Canada. Microfossil G and H is *Eospheria tyleri*, a form observed in many iron formations and believed to have been instrumental in the production of iron formation.

Archean Greenstone Belts

Archean strata is usually associated with what are known as greenstone belts. Greenstone is metamorphosed basalt (which turns green upon being "cooked"). This basalt also often shows what are known as pillows. Pillows were formed when the basalt was extruded onto the ocean floor; this is associated with what are known as "island arcs" in plate tectonics. Island arcs represent the initial stages in the formation of continental crust. Most island arc sediments were (or are) deposited in waters of the open ocean and not in the shallow water associated with continental crust. This partially explains the scarcity of distinct stromatolites in Archean iron formations, as they normally don't grow where there is little sunlight available for photosynthesis. As a consequence, Archean greenstone belts contain iron formation of the Algoma-type.

Archean Laminar Stromatolites

Besides commonly being dark hued, many Archean stromatolites occur with a distinctive type of laminar structure with a distinctive "signature" composed of regular,

Figure 4-11. Outcrop of greenstone in the Ely Greenstone Belt of northern Minnesota. Greenstone is metamorphosed basalt. Greenstone Belts are representative of some of the earth's oldest rocks and terrains; Algoma-type iron formation is associated with them.

Figure 4-12. "Pillows" (at left) in basalt associated with an Archean Greenstone belt in western Ontario.

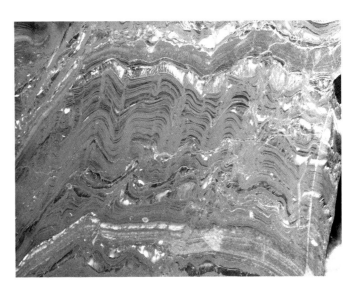

Figure 4-13. "Fingers" emanating from a finely laminated and colorful stromatolite in the late Archean Hamersley Iron Formation of Western Australia. Iron-rich stromatolitic laminae shown here are forming what could be considered as stromatolitic digitate "fingers." Specimens like this have been widely distributed through the fossil show in Tucson, Arizona.

Figure 4-14. Strelley Pool stromatolite. This exhibits a weathered surface of laminar stromatolite that came from 3.4 b.y. old strata of the Pilbara Block of western Australia. Originally they were (probably) black or gray, but in the dry climate of western Australia some oxidization has occurred to convert them to this tan color.

equally spaced laminae. This "signature" is well demonstrated by the Strelley Pool stromatolites that come from early Archean strata of Western Australia's Pilbara Block. Strelley Pool stromatolites are currently the world's oldest fossils, dating about 3.5 billion years. All or most of these occurrences appear to be associated with greenstone belts. The Pilbara Block does, however, include some continental crust—a rare Archean occurrence!

Some Precambrian workers have questioned the biogenicity of Archean laminar stromatolites (Lowe 2011). This skepticism appears unwarranted since these oldest of stromatolites exhibit most of the same signatures found in younger ones. Such skepticism suggests decades-old science that viewed all Precambrian stromatolites with suspicion—before microfossils of the Proterozoic Gunflint Formation vindicated their biogenicity. Archean stromatolites of various types represent the clearest and most secure evidence for the great antiquity of life on planet Earth!

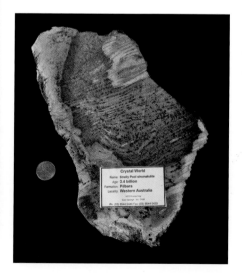

Figure 4-15. Strelley Pool laminar stromatolite, Western Australia. A polished slab of what is one of the oldest fossils known to date, early Archean.

Figure 4-16. Another large chunk of a Strelley Pool "strom" from Western Australia's Pilbara Block. The red color is from the pervasive red (iron oxide) soil of Australia's outback. The label is from an Australian dealer in geocollectibles who has distributed these ancient fossils.

Figure 4-17. A beautiful polished slab of the oldest known stromatolite/fossil in the world. Archean stromatolite from an incredible 3.49 b.y.a. This awe-inspiring ancient laminar stromatolite comes from the Dresser Formation, North Pole, west of Marble Bar in the Pilbara region of Western Australia.

Figure 4-20. Laminar stromatolites from near Thunder Bay, Ontario, with amethyst crystals.

Figure 4-18. Laminar stromatolites from Archean strata near Schreiber, western Ontario. These are similar to Strelley Pool "stroms," but are still in the reduced (unoxidized) state typical of many Archean stromatolites and sediments.

Figure 4-21. Cut and polished surface of laminar stromatolite with amethyst crystals from near Thunder Bay, Ontario.

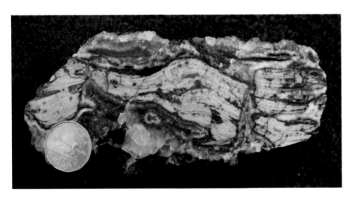

Figure 4-19. What are believed to be laminar stromatolites from Archean strata near Thunder Bay (Pearl, Ontario), western Ontario. Amethyst crystals are well-known in late Archean granite near Thunder Bay. Archean cherts have been injected by this same granite. Some yield these banded patterns, which the authors interpret as laminar stromatolites. These are similar to the laminar "stroms" found near Schreiber, Ontario and probably came from strata of the same age.

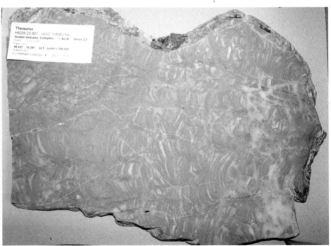

Figure 4-22. Abitibi Greenstone Belt stromatolite, Joutel Quebec, Canada. Deep-sea Archean rocks exposed during mineral exploration activity contained transported blocks of Archean limestone that contained stromatolites like this. This limestone and associated "stroms" formed originally in shallow water of the shelf of a small ancestral landmass in what is known as a greenstone belt. Greenstone Belts and their volcanic rocks represent the initial stages of continental crust formation. The Abitibi Greenstone Belt is one of many greenstone belts in the Superior Province of the vast Canadian Shield. *Photo courtesy of Anthony Howell, Redpath Museum, McGill University, Montreal, Quebec*

Distribution of Archean Stromatolites

Archean stromatolites are known mainly from Western Australia, sub-Saharan Africa (Zimbabwe, Democratic Republic of the Congo formerly known as Zaire, and Swaziland), North America (Canadian Shield), Wyoming, and Russia. Western Australian occurrences in the Pilbara Block appear to be the oldest. Radiometric age dates of these are in the 3.5 billion year range.

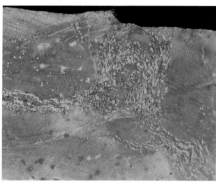

Figure 4-23. Pyrrhotite-replaced stromatolite of the form genus *Thassanites* sp. preserved in siderite-rich iron formation of the Michipicoten Group near Wawa, Ontario. These are one of the most unusual of Archean stromatolite occurrences. Sliced specimen from the Helen Iron Formation of the Late Archean Michipicoten Group, where it was mined prior to 2003 from an underground mine working siderite beds.

Figure 4-24. Another slice through the stromatolite form genus *Thassanites*, from the Archean Michipicoten Group at Wawa, Ontario.

Figure 4-25. Large chunk of sideritic dolomite from the late Archean Michipicoten Group at Wawa, Ontario, which contains stromatolites of the form genus *Thassanites*. Specimen in the Royal Ontario Museum, Toronto, Ontario.

Figure 4-26. Stromatolite of probable Archean age from a large glacial erratic found in northeastern Missouri. This was associated with glacial till containing a predominance of Archean erratics consisting of greenstone and gneiss. This boulder may have come from now-buried outcrops of Archean strata in northern Minnesota or western Ontario.

Figure 4-27. This is probably a brecciated laminar stromatolite of Archean age found as a glacial erratic near Minocqua, Wisconsin. Without the fracturing, this would be a laminar stromatolite similar to the Strelley Pool "stroms," a type of stromatolite characteristic of the Archean. Stromatolites (and other fossils) can occur in glacial erratics whose outcrops were covered by glacial sediments during the Pleistocene ice age. Moving glaciers can "pluck" and transport boulders like that from which this slice was taken. Piles of glacial boulders and cobbles sometimes yield interesting and surprising specimens.

Stromatolites from Glacial Boulders

In the northern hemisphere, Precambrian stromatolites can sometimes be found far from outcrops where they originated, a result of being carried as glacial boulders and deposited as glacial erratics. Sometimes the actual outcrops from which they originated no longer exist, having been covered by glacial drift.

Steep Rock Lake Ontario Stromatolites

Some of the largest and most spectacular Early Precambrian stromatolites occur in the former iron mines at Steep Rock Lake near the town of Atikokan, Ontario. Here, late Archean limestone contains what are some of the planets largest "stroms" exposed to view by former mining operations.

Figure 4-28. A large stromatolite-bearing glacial erratic near Grandview, Wisconsin, plucked and carried by ice age glaciers from Archean or early Proterozoic strata some five miles from where it originated. Smaller glacial erratics like those in the previous two photos were possibly carried hundreds of miles from outcrops where they originated.

Figure 4-29. Large (immense for the Archean) stromatolites in the former Steep Rock Iron mine near Atikokan, western Ontario. Draining the water of Steep Rock mining operations exposed what are some of the world's largest, oldest, and most spectacular stromatolites. These are also probably the most spectacular examples of the planet's early life. The stromatolite-bearing layers have been tilted from tectonic forces placing the gigantic domal "stroms" at an angle. *Photo courtesy of Tom Nash*

Figure 4-30. The east arm of Steep Rock Lake, the site of a large, inactive iron mine near Atikokan, western Ontario.

Figure 4-31. Stromatolite-bearing layers along the edge of Steep Rock Lake, which is still filling and will eventually cover these outcrops and the giant "stroms" of the previous photo. *Photo courtesy of Tom Nash*

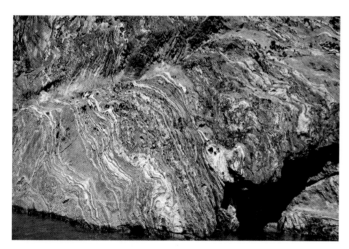

Figure 4-32. Stromatolitic limestone exposed along the current shore of Steep Rock Lake, Atikokan, Ontario. *Photo courtesy of Tom Nash*

Figure 4-33. Glaciated surface of stromatolites and stromatolitic limestone exposed along Steep Rock Lake, Atikokan, Ontario.

Figure 4-34. Close-up of glacially abraded stromatolites and stromatolitic limestone along Steep Rock Lake, Atikokan, Ontario.

Figure 4-35. Cut and polished digitate stromatolites from the Steep Rock locality.

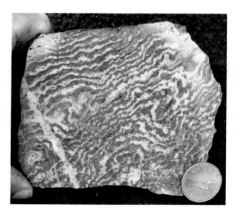

Figure 4-36. Laminar stromatolite, Steep Rock Lake, western Ontario. Archean limestones of late Archean age crop out near the western Ontario town of Atikokan, where they are associated with what are believed to be shallow water deposits around an island arc. This slab came from one of the large Steep Rock domal stromatolites.

North American Archean Stromatolite Occurrences

Large portions of North America are underlaid by Archean rocks, most of which consist of high-grade metamorphic rocks like gneiss and schist. Beds of iron formation, black slate, and hard beds of limestone or dolomite can be found scattered locally through these ancient rocks. Almost without exception, these Archean rocks will be hard and somewhat metamorphosed and appear most unpromising for yielding fossils. As with other Precambrian regions of the globe like sub-Saharan Africa and Australia,

North America is made up of a mosaic of different geologic provinces, each one formed during a particular range of geologic time—some very ancient, others not as old. Superior Province is the largest of the North American Archean provinces. The ancient Slave Province in the northwestern portion of the Canadian Shield is smaller. The eastern Nane Province of southwestern Greenland is the oldest, and the Wyoming Province of the western United States is the second oldest.

Figure 4-37. Late Archean stromatolite-bearing pink limestone or marble in the Hartville Uplift near Guernsey, Wyoming.

Figure 4-38. Stromatolites in a boulder of Archean limestone near Guernsey, Wyoming.

Figure 4-39. Weathered surface of a *Cryptozoan*-like stromatolite from Late Archean strata of the Hartville Uplift, western Wyoming.

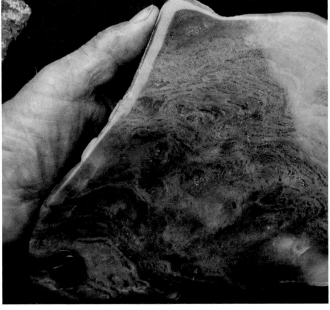

Figure 4-40. Slice through the same stromatolite but with a cut and polished surface.

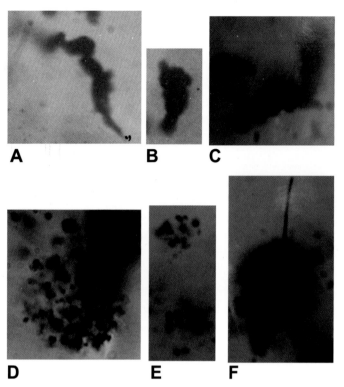

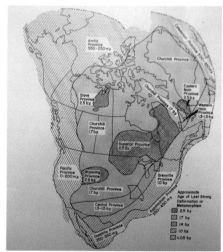

Figure 4-42. Stromatolite from the mid-Archean Bulawayan Limestone of Zimbabwe. Until 1990, these and similar stromatolites with microfossils from the Democratic Republic of the Congo, formerly known as Zaire, were the oldest known fossils. Like many other Archean "stroms," they are dark colored because they formed in a reducing environment.

Figure 4-41. Microfossils[?] from Archean black chert of the Ferris Mountains, Wyoming.

Figure 4-43. Fragment of Fig Tree stromatolite. A variety of bacteria-like fossils were found in black cherts of the mid Archean Fig Tree Formation of Swaziland. Swaziland is a gold-producing country that occupies a massif (uplifted area of ancient rock) in South Africa. Its Archean rocks are gold-bearing, as they are in many other greenstone belts around the globe. Microfossils in black chert of the Fig Tree and Ovenwacht Series were some of the first-described Archean fossils.

Figure 4-43a. Red Lake Metasediments (Schopf 2006). These 2.925 b.y. old stromatolites occur in an Archean greenstone belt in a remote part of Ontario, Canada. They are some of the oldest known "stroms" of the Canadian Shield. *Photo courtesy of Bow Narrows Camp, Red Lake, Ontario, Canada*

Figure 4-44. Precambrian Provinces of North America. The Archean provinces are shown in pink. Archean rock may be prevalent in these provinces; however, younger rocks may cover them to a major extent. The Paleoproterozoic Churchill Province is one of the largest of the North American Precambrian Provinces. Note that along the margins of the continent occur the areas of youngest mountain building (tectonism) and thus some of the youngest rocks.

Glossary

Anaerobic bacteria or anaerobes. Bacteria (microbes) that cannot tolerate the presence of elemental or free oxygen.

Free oxygen. This is the elemental oxygen in the planet's atmosphere. Elemental oxygen is a by-product of photosynthesis, which originally was a toxic gas to microbes; today it is still toxic to anaerobes.

Gneiss and schist. High grade, crystalline metamorphic rocks which formed by high pressure deep within the earth's crust from sedimentary rock such as shale and siltstone. These hard crystalline rocks are especially characteristic of the Archean Era.

Greenstone belts. Sequences of strata made up of Algoma-type iron formation, black slate, or phyllite interbedded with layers of basalt, the basalt often exhibiting "pillows" from being deposited on the sea floor in deep water. Greenstone belts constitute some of the earth's oldest rocks.

High-grade metamorphic rocks. Rocks that have been severely changed by a combination of deep burial and associated heating. They are usually composed of noticeable crystals.

Iron Formation. A unique sedimentary rock composed of hematite, jasper (or jaspellite) and microcrystalline quartz. Iron formation is now believed to have been formed from biogenic activity; it sometimes can contain distinctive microfossils as well as stromatolites.

Methane. Natural gas, a compound of four hydrogen and one carbon atom and one of the simplest organic compounds. Methane is believed to have been an early component of the earth's (Hadean) atmosphere.

Photic zone. That portion of the water in the ocean or a large lake where light is capable of penetrating.

Radiometric age dating. A method of geologic age dating which gives a numerical age date and which appears to be relatively accurate. It is based upon the fact that radioactive elements are unstable and decompose (because they are radioactive) into a decay product that accumulates with the passage of time. A radioactive age date (geochron) is obtained by comparing the amount of decay product with the amount of parent radioactive element in a sample--the more decay product, the older the sample.

Reducing atmosphere. A planetary atmosphere containing no elemental oxygen but which might contain methane and thus promote an anaerobic environment for early life.

Reducing conditions. Conditions on a planet which would exist with the presence of methane in the planetary atmosphere and which would promote an anaerobic environment for early life.

Subduction or subduction zones. The dragging of part of the earth's crust back into the lithosphere (the crust and uppermost layer of the mantle). The existence of subduction zones forms a major part of the concept of plate tectonics.

Bibliography

Buick, Roger. 1990. "Microfossil recognition in Archean rocks: an appraisal of spheroids and filaments from 3500 m.y. old chert-barite unit at North Pole, Western Australia." *Palaios*, 5:441-459.

Cloud, Preston. 1973. "Pseudofossils: a plea for caution." *Geology*, 1:123-127.

Hofmann, Hans J. and Mario Masson. 1994. "Archean stromatolites from Abitibi greenstone belt, Quebec, Canada." *Bulletin of the Geological Society of America*, 106: 424-429.

Hofmann, Hans J., R. P. Sage, and E. N. Berdusco. 1991. "Archean stromatolites in Michipicoten Group siderite ore at Wawa, Ontario." *Economic Geology*, 86:1023-1030.

Hofmann, Hans J. 1996. "Precambrian fossil occurrences in North America: an overview and appraisal of the data." In J. E. Repetski (ed.), Sixth North American Paleontological Convention, Abstracts of Papers, Paleontological Society, Special Publication No. 8, p. 172.

Knoll, Andrew H. 1992. "The early evolution of eukaryotes: a geological perspective." *Science*, 256:622-627.

LaBerge, Gene L. 1967. "Microfossils and Precambrian iron formation." *Geological Society of America Bulletin*, 78:331-342.

Lowe, Donald R. 1980. "Stromatolites 3,400-Myr old from the Archean of Western Australia." *Nature*, 284:441-443.

Lowe, Donald R. 1995. "Abiological origin of described stromatolites older than 3.2 Ga." *Geology* 23:191-192.

Schopf, J. William, and B. M. Packer. 1987. "Early Archean (3.3-billion to 3.5-billion-year-old) microfossils from Warrawoona Group, Australia." *Science*, 237:70-73.

Stinchcomb, Bruce L., and Christopher Baught. 2008. "Morphology of stromatolites from a presumed Archean Glacial Boulder from Lewis County, Missouri." (abstract). Proceedings of the 2008 Missouri Academy of Sciences Meeting, Geology/Geophysics Section.

Walsh, Maud M., and Donald R. Lowe. 1985. "Filamentous microfossils from the 3,500-Myr-old Onverwacht Group, Barberton Mountain Land, South Africa." *Nature*, 314:530-532.

Chapter Five

Stromatolites Through Time and Around the Globe

B. L. Stinchcomb

Fossil stromatolites occur widely over the globe, as can be seen with a cursory look at this chapter. Noticeable in this chapter also is that it is somewhat of a compendium of stromatolites; note the word somewhat, since fossil stromatolite occurrences worldwide are extensive and any attempt at any sort of inclusive coverage would be nothing but facetious. The limits of what is presented here was determined by what was available to the authors and was not too repetitious. Stromatolites, like other fossils (as well as minerals) are available from a variety of sources. They often can be collected in the field, a method by which some can get "hooked" on these fascinating objects. Self-collecting has the potential, if one gets especially familiar with the rocks, of producing forms that otherwise would rarely be seen and might even yield a type or occurrence new to science. As John Pojeta stated, "the more eyes looking for fossils, the better for paleontology, as this increases the likelihood of some previously unknown types being found." It should, however, be mentioned that most stromatolites in the rough are not very striking or attractive. They must be correctly oriented, cut, lapped, and polished to bring out their structure.

Many of the more spectacular stromatolites are distributed through mineral and fossil dealers at mineral, rock, and fossil fairs that have replaced the roadside rock shop of a few decades past. Stromatolites and other fossils and minerals that show up at such "rock fairs" can originate from around the globe, and unlike "stroms" that might be self-collected, generally are cut and polished, a procedure that can be difficult and time consuming.

Some, however, have criticized commerce in rocks, minerals, and fossils with regard to learning about stromatolites (as well as other geo-collectibles). With self-collecting, for example, ownership enables a real "hands on" approach to learning, which is most effective since it typically becomes permanent knowledge. Limiting the interested public's access to self-collecting is really putting up a roadblock to learning. This roadblock is usually based upon the erroneous comparison of paleontology to archeology. In this light it should be mentioned that stromatolites usually are not that rare, and unlike the cultural objects of archeology, they occur as parts of rock strata that usually extends over a large area. Attempts to regulate or prohibit their acquisition under the guise of rarity is usually ridiculous.

Stromatolites from the Cambrian Period to the present (the Phanerozoic Eon) in general look similar to those of the Precambrian but with one very significant difference. Phanerozoic stromatolites often have animal and plant life intimately associated with them. This is important since stromatolite colonies and moneran mats may have been the environments in which the first animal and plant life developed, evolved and prospered.

R. J. Leis

This chapter is an excursion into the land of fossilized stromatolites. The photos are from the Archean to the present and come from localities around the globe. Fossilized stromatolites are some of the most abundant and enduring fossils on Earth and are found worldwide. Many of the photos in this chapter exhibit polished stromatolite slabs that really bring out their beauty. These stromatolites, like others, were produced by microbes, some of which date back 3.5 billion years. While the microbes that produced these beautiful stromatolites are usually no longer present in the fossils, the distinctive patterns that they form shows that life was once there. These fossilized stromatolites help reveal details about the earth's early environment.

Some of the stromatolites shown in this chapter have been metamorphosed—that is, they have been heated and subjected to pressure while being buried for millions of years in the earth. Even after being metamorphosed and crystallized, many of these stromatolites still exhibit classic patterns and are quite beautiful.

We don't have any photos of stromatolites from other planets, but we might someday, especially Mars. NASA is extensively studying fossilized stromatolites to help them ascertain if life forms responsible for them might once have existed on Mars. Some NASA paleobiologists believe that since many fossilized stromatolites formed here on earth under harsh and extreme environmental conditions that may have been similar to Mars' early environment, it's possible that microbial life forms once lived on Mars or perhaps even still exist today.

Indeed, Mary E. White, in her book *Earth Alive! From Microbes to a Living Planet* suggests there is a possible stromatolite site on Mars. Dr. White states that in the area called Tera Sabacea, within the rim of a crater that hasn't been named near the Martian equator, an outcrop with an area of about 77 square miles (200 km2) may be of stromatolitic origin.

Over the past several years, NASA has been actively studying stromatolites on Earth as it seeks to find traces of life on other planets, in the hope that these explorations will enhance our understanding of the origins, evolution, and distribution of life in the universe. NASA believes that, based on what it has observed here on Earth, our biosphere began soon after the earth's formation, and that the same may have occurred elsewhere, especially on Mars. The fact that liquid water once existed on Mars and that planetary systems may be common in the universe suggests that life might also have existed, or still does, on other planets. NASA believes that the search for habitable planets depends on identifying the distribution of life-sustaining environments in our solar system and beyond. Earth is dominated by microbes both in terms of biomass and the length of time they were present here. Bacteria have been and are the dominant forms of life on Earth. Almost 80 percent of the history of life on Earth is the history of microbial life, including stromatolites. Microbes exhibit, to us and NASA, strategies for existing over very long periods of time here on Earth and perhaps on other planets, too.

Will fossilized stromatolites ever be found on Mars? We will just have to hope and wait. Martian stromatolites may be a long shot, but we certainly believe that their presence is possible.

Even without Martian stromatolites, we have more than enough earthly examples to fill this chapter. So sit back, relax, enjoy, and let your eyes feast on stromatolites through time and around the globe.

Figure 5-1. On August 6, 2012, Curiosity, NASA's Mars rover, landed on Mars. Ever since, Curiosity has been searching for indications that life once existed on the planet. NASA describes this as a photo taken by the navigation camera on Curiosity's mast, looking back after finishing a drive of 328 feet on the 548th Martian day, 2/19/2014. The rows of rock to the right of the fresh wheel tracks are an outcrop called "Junda." The rows form striations on the ground, a characteristic seen in images of this area taken from orbit. *Image from NASA website*

Figure 5-2. As described on the NASA website, this mosaic of images from Curiosity's mast camera shows geological members of the Yellowknife Bay formation. The Sheepbed mudstone in the foreground rises up through Gillespie Lake member to the Point Lake outcrop. These rocks record superimposed ancient lake and stream deposits that offered past environmental conditions favorable for microbial life. Wind erosion exposed the rocks hereabout 70 million years ago. *NASA/JPL-Caltech/MSSS*

Proterozoic Eon—2.5 billion years ago to 542 million years ago

Figure 5-3. Stromatolitic iron formation (Tiger iron). Hamersley Range, Western Australia. A widely distributed stromatolite and rockhound item. Banded iron is covered in Chapter 3.

Figure 5-5. Paleoproterozoic. By around 2 b.y.a. rising oxygen levels would have begun to turn the oceans and sky from red to blue. This painting illustrates what the sky might have looked like at this time as the atmosphere became infused with oxygen. Stromatolites would have formed along all the land mass shorelines and they, along with other photosynthetic monerans, would create the great oxygenation event. The earth's protective ozone shield would also be forming at this time.

Figure 5-4. Laminar Archean stromatolites. The black slab is from Schreiber, western Ontario; the "eggs" are made from identical but oxidized laminar "stroms" from the Hamersley Range of Western Australia. This type of stromatolite is characteristic of the late Archean.

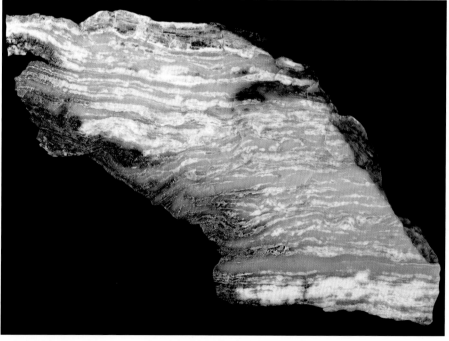

Figure 5-6. Stromatolite from the Bad River Dolomite, late Archean or early Paleoproterozoic. Bayfield County, Wisconsin. Wisconsin's oldest fossil!

Figure 5-7. *Hadrophycus immanus*, Early Proterozoic, Libby Super Group, Libby Flats, Medicine Bow Range, Wyoming. Stromatolites from this area are highly metamorphosed and extremely variable in appearance.

Figure 5-9. *Kinneyia simulans* (mottled moneran mat? or printstone). McRae Shale, late Archean 2.5 b.y. or early Paleoproterozoic, 2.49 b.y. Hamersley Range, Western Australia. Some have stated that these are just Leisegang Rings; however, almost identical structures originally described by Charles B. Walcott occur in unoxidized strata of the Belt Series of Montana.

Figure 5-10. *Pilbara perplexia*. Oxidized form. Duck Creek Dolomite, Ashburton Basin, Western Australia.

Figure 5-8. Stromatolite in talc, *Kussiella* sp., Early Proterozoic 2.3–2.4 b.y., Noondine chert, Commberdale sub group, Three Springs, Western Australia.

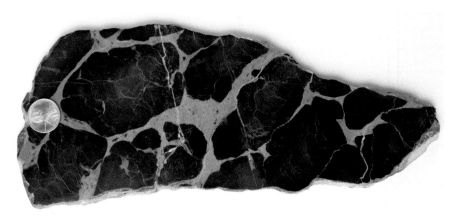

Figure 5-11. *Pilbara perplexa*. An example of this nice "strom" from a more oxidized environment. Duck Creek Dolomite, Wyloo Group, Ashburton Basin, Western Australia.

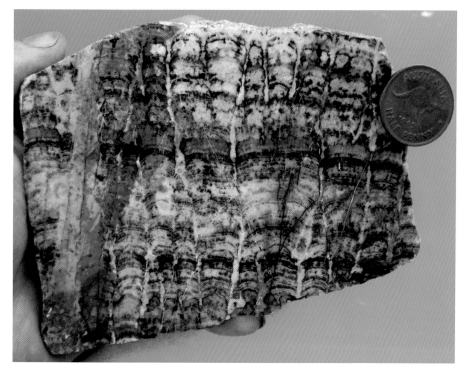

Figure 5-13. *Eucapsiphora leakensis* (1.6-2.1 b.y.) Small branching "stroms" from the Mount Leake Sandstone, Earaheedy Group, Earaheedy Basin, near Meekatharre, Western Australia.

Figure 5-12. *Asperia ashburtonia*. Duck Creek Dolomite, (2.4 b.y.) Wyloo Group, Ashburton Basin near Paraburdoo, Pilbara Range, Western Australia. Characterized by closely packed columns.

Figure 5-15. Marbleized laminar "strom." Early Proterozoic, Kolmarden, Sweden.

Figure 5-16. Marbleized stromatolite. Early Proterozoic (2.2–2.4 b.y.). Randville Dolomite, near Randville, northern Michigan.

Figure 5-14. *Yelma digitata*. Yelma Formation, Earaheedy Group, Nabberu or Earaheedy Basin, Western Australia.

Figure 5-17. Kona Dolomite stromatolite. A variety of attractive stromatolites and oncolites occur in the 2.1-2.3 b.y. old Kona Dolomite of northern Michigan. These are covered in detail in chapter eight.

Figure 5-18. *Collenia undosa.* (Mary Ellen Jasper). These attractive stromatolites from the 1.8-1.9 b.y. old Biwabik Formation of northern Minnesota's Mesabi Range have been widely circulated through rockhounds. They are covered more completely in chapter 8.

Figure 5-20. *Erraheedia kuleliensis* (1.7 b.y.). Kulele Limestone, Wiluna, Western Australia.

Figure 5-19. Gunflint stromatolite (close relative of Mary Ellen Jasper), 1.8–2.0 b.y. old, near Kakabeka Falls, Ontario, Canada. The Gunflint has yielded a variety of microfossils associated with its stromatolites, and the presence of these microfossils convinced geologists that very ancient stromatolites in the rock record were indeed of biogenic origin.

Figure 5-21. Mesoproterozoic. By around 1.5 b.y.a. enough oxygen would have entered the atmosphere to turn the oceans and sky blue as you see it in this stromatolite mural. Multi-celled life, if it existed at all, would have been limited and very primitive, leaving little fossil record of its existence. From 1.5 b.y.a. to 800 m.y.a. stromatolites would have been at their maximum diversity worldwide. The earth's protective ozone shield would allow life to go forward and exist on land. *Courtesy of Chase Studios/Terry Chase*

Figure 5-22. Black and white Russian stromatolite. Village Torgo, Southern Yakutia, Russia.

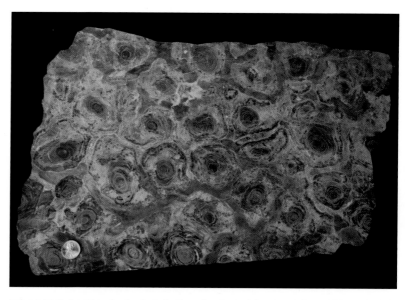

Figure 5-23. *Gianophyton gargarnicus.* Upper river Bakson, village of Bakson, Eastern Sayan, Russia.

Figure 5-24. Horizontal section (or view) of a Mongolian, Precambrian stromatolite, a striking and colorful stromatolite. Grene, Mongolia.

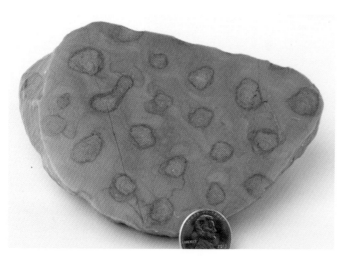

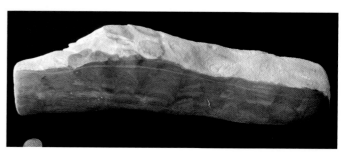

Figure 5-26. *Collenia* sp. Tranverse section. (Chinese Flower-ring-rock stromatolite). Northeast Red Formation. These "stroms" are quarried and used extensively as decorative stone in China, including on building facades in Tiananmen Square. Mid Proterozoic, China.

Figure 5-25. Digitate Precambrian stromatolite from Durkincal, Burkina Faso, Africa.

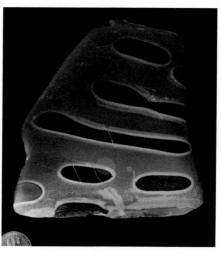

5-29. *Copperia tubiformis* Walcott (Zebra Rock). Western Australia

Figure 5-27. *Collenia* sp. Horizontal (top) section. A commercial tile of Chinese Flower-ring-rock, northeast red. Mid Proterozoic.

Figure 5-28. *Copperia tubiformis* Walcott. (Zebra Rock) Ranford Formation, Kununurra, East Kimberly Range, Western Australia.

Figure 5-30. *Copperia tubiformis* Walcott. From western Montana, Belt Series, Newland Limestone, Townsend, Montana.

Figure 5-31. *Newlandia concentrica* Walcott. One of the many peculiar stromatolites described by Charles Walcott from the Mid Proterozoic Belt Series in the Belt Mountains of Montana. Newland Limestone, Belt Series, Big Belt Mountains, near Townsend, Montana.

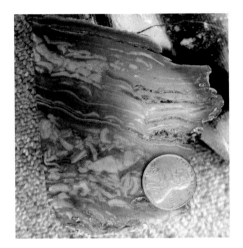

Figure 5-32. *Ozarkcollenia laminata*. Mid Proterozoic (1.5 b.y.). Ketcherside Tuff, Cuthbertson Mountain, Iron County, Missouri.

Figure 5-33. *Ozarkcollenia laminata* Stinchcomb. Mid Proterozoic, southern Missouri.

Figure 5-34. *Collenia sp.*, Altyn Limestone, Belt Series, Mid Proterozoic, Essex, Montana

Figure 5-35. Stromatolitic limestone. Wickenburg, Arizona. Mid Proterozoic. Correlates with the Grand Canyon Series of the Grand Canyon and the Belt Series of Montana, Idaho, and British Columbia.

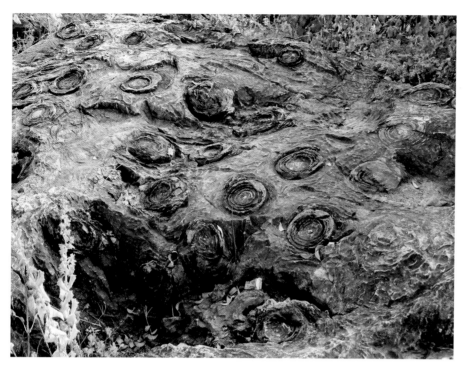

Figure 5-37. Mid-Proterozoic stromatolite, Tegana Formation, Ouarzazate, Atlas Mountains, Morocco, Africa.

Figure 5-38. Mid-Proterozoic stromatolite, 1.2 b.y.a. Anti-Atlas Mountains, Morocco, Africa.

Figure 5-36. Salkhan Fossil Park contains Mesoproterozoic stromatolites of approximately 1.5 b.y.a. This park is in the Salkhan village in Sonebhadra district of Eastern Uttar Prodesh, India. The park is an important scientific asset to India, and, indeed, the world, and deserves to be protected and preserved. *Photo courtesy of D.C. Kumar, taken at Salkhan fossils park, Robertganj distt. Sonbhadra (u.p.), India*

Figure 5-39. Mid-Proterozoic approximately 1.2 b.y.a. stromatolite, Mescal Limestone, Apache group from the Desert Museum, west of Tucson, Arizona. The green color may be due to the presence of copper.

Figure 5-40. Precambrian, Zagora region, Morocco, Africa.

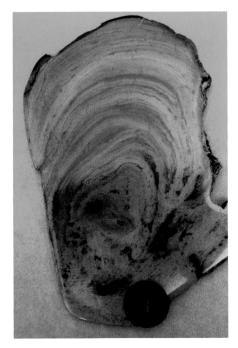

Figure 5-41. *Baicalia capricornia*, Irregully Formation (1.2 b.y.). Bunge Mall Basin, Ashburton River, Kooline Staton, Western Australia.

Figure 5-42. *Baicalia capricornia,* Oxidized form. Irregully Formation, Ashburton River, Western Australia.

Figure 5-43. *Baicalia capricornia.* Reduced (green) form. Irregully Formation, Ashburton River, Kooline Station, Western Australia.

Figure 5-44. *Inzeria intia.* Bitter Springs Formation (800 m.y.) Adelaide Geosyncline, Alice Springs area, Northern Territory, Australia.

Figure 5-47. *Boxonia pertaknurra.* Rough unpolished side of this Late Precambrian stromatolite. Bitter Springs Formation, Adelaide Geosyncline, Northern Territory, Australia.

Figure 5-45. *Acaciella australica.* Bitter Springs Formation, SE of Alice Springs, Northern Territory, Australia.

Figure 5-46. *Acaciella australica.* Bitter Springs Formation, Adelaide Geosyncline, southeast of Alice Springs, Northern Territory, Australia.

Figure 5-48. *Boxonia pertaknurra.* Polished side of previous stromatolite. Bitter Springs Formation (800 m.y.), Adelaide Geosyncline, Alice Springs area, Northern Territory, Australia.

Figure 5-49. *Linella avis.* Bitter Springs Formation, near Alice Springs, Northern Territory, Australia.

Figure 5-50. *Kulparia alicia.* Bitter Springs Formation, Alice Springs, Northern Teritory, Australia.

Figure 5-51. Ocherous stromatolite. Thought to be Neoproterozoic, Little Grassy Mountain, Madison County, Missouri.

Figure 5-53. Ocherous Laminar stromatolite. Neoproterozoic, Womack, Missouri.

Figure 5-54. *Baicalia* cf. *burra*. Neoproterozoic, Julius River, Trowutta, Tasmania.

Figure 5-55. Stromatolite. Neoproterozoic, Deep Springs Formation, eastern California, near Mount Dunfee.

Figure 5-52. Ocherous stromatolite. Thought to be Neoproterozoic, Womack, Missouri. Associated with diatremes of Devonian age from which masses of these were probably brought up from the subsurface.

Figure 5-56. Neoproterozoic. From about 800 to about 550 m.y.a. Eukaryotic life forms began to appear in the world's oceans such as those depicted in this painting. *Ediacara*, a late Precambrian life form attached to the sea floor, lives in the shallow water where stromatolites dominate the underwater shallows. Green algae mixing with tidal silt cling to stromatolites. Brown algae drift in the movement of wave currents. "Jellyfish" are grouped together in the top left of this scene and a disc-shaped *Dickinsonia* lying on the sandy floor exists with these and other multi-celled species at this time …then next comes the Cambrian!

Cambrian Period—541 to 486 million years ago

Figure 5-57. Cambrian. From this point on, stromatolites began to decline worldwide due to predators and a series of ice ages. New life forms began to appear in abundance. This painting depicts shafts of sunlight penetrating the water inundating the stromatolites in this tidal zone. Undulating flexible lobes on the sides of its body enable the *anomalocaris* to glide through water while searching for its favorite trilobite munchies. Life in this time period excels in populating the aquatic earth.

Figure 5-58. Cambrian mollusks that were intimately associated with digitate "stroms" are seen here. This is strictly a Phanerozoic phenomena. Cambrian, Missouri Ozarks. The stromatolites are now represented by holes through which pencils have been inserted.

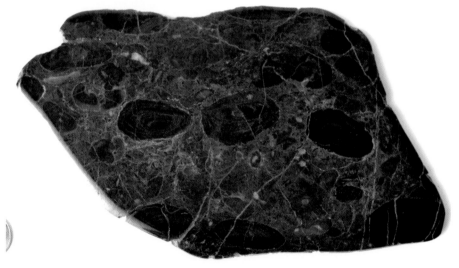

Figure 5-59. Oncolite. *Girvanella* sp. Lower Cambrian, Chambless Limestone. Marble Mountains, Southern California.

Figure 5-60. Oncolites. Lower Cambrian, Ruin Wash, Pioche Shale, eastern Nevada.

Figure 5-61. Oncolites. *Girvanella* sp. Lower Cambrian, Carrera Formation, near Rachel, Nevada, adjacent to Area 51.

Figure 5-62. Metamorphosed stromatolite (marble). Lower Cambrian, Bido, Norland, Norway. The evidence of a stromatolite has been almost totally obliterated by metamorphism.

Figure 5-63. Weathered "strom" with aurichalcite. Hidden Treasure Mine, Ophir District, Tooele County, Utah.

Figure 5-64. *Girvanella* sp. Oncolites. Cambrian, Coosa River, Alabama.

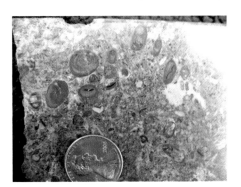

Figure 5-65. *Girvanella* sp. Small oncolites, some with trilobite fragments forming a nucleus. Bonneterre Formation, St. Francois County, Missouri.

Figure 5-66. Stromatolite, Little Falls Dolomite, Herkimer County near Middleville, New York.

Figure 5-67. Close-up of stromatolite with Herkimer diamond and black anthroxolite, Herkimer County, New York. The so-called Herkimer diamonds of upstate New York (clear quartz crystals) are associated with stromatolites in the Cambrian age Little Falls Dolomite. Stromatolites in the Cambrian appear in some way to encourage the formation of quartz crystals, probably in their producing cavities in which the crystals can grow after the stromatolite reef becomes rock in the earth's crust. Quartz crystals in the form of quartz druse is also a common phenomena associated with stromatolites of the Cambrian Potosi Formation of the Missouri Ozarks, which strangely is of identical geological age as the Little Falls Dolomite of New York.

Figure 5-68. Quartz druse, a coating of fine crystals, formed with and associated with Cambrian stromatolites. These can be common in the Cambrian Potosi Formation of the Missouri Ozarks. These rounded masses of quartz (quartz druse or mineral blossoms) are found associated with domal and digitate stromatolites. Their formation appears to have been affected in some way by the presence of stromatolites.

Figure 5-69. Digitate stromatolites, Upper Cambrian, Arbuckle Mountains, Oklahoma.

Figure 5-70. *Cryptozoon proliferium* Hall. Little Falls Dolomite, Upper Cambrian, Saratoga Springs, New York.

Figure 5-71. Stromatolite (Zebra marble) Upper Cambrian, Notch Creek Formation, Millard County, Utah.

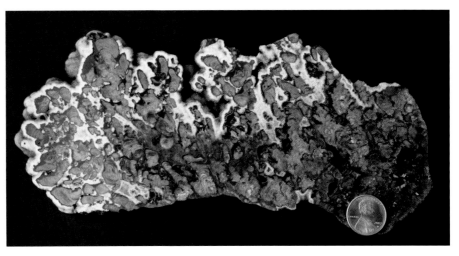

Figure 5-72. *Madiganites mawsoni.* Middle Cambrian, Top Springs Limestone, Katherine, Northern Territory, Australia.

Figure 5-73. Stromatolite replaced with anglesite, Cambrian, Cochise County, Gleeson, Arizona.

Figure 5-74. *Conophytum basalticum.* Antrim Basalt, Katherine, Northern Territory, Australia. A "strom" that occurs in silicified limestone interbedded with basalts.

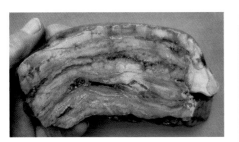

Figure 5-75. Domal stromatolite preserved in chert. Eminence Formation, Upper Cambrian, St. Francois County, Missouri.

Figure 5-76. *Conophyton* sp. Side view showing nested cones. Eminence Formation, Upper Cambrian, Womack, Missouri. Associated with the St. Genevieve Fault System.

Ordovician Period—485 to 445 million years ago

Figure 5-77. Ordovician. During this primeval time a rainstorm at low tide reveals an abandoned nautiloid cephalopod shell resting on this foundation of stromatolites. Starfish cling to the mass of stromatolites that thrive in this shallow bay.

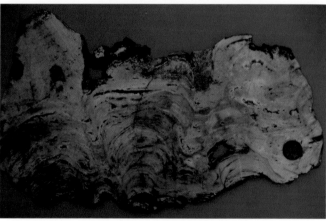

Figure 5-78. *Cryptozoan* sp. A vertical slice through a large stromatolite from the *Cryptozoan* reef of the Missouri Ozarks. This stromatolitic marker bed extends over a large portion of the Missouri Ozarks, where it occurs near the bottom of sequences of Ordovician strata. "Stroms" were still very prevalent in the earliest part of the Ordovician, which includes the Gasconade Formation of the Missouri Ozarks.

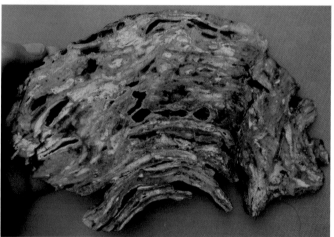

Figure 5-79. Another slice through a domal stromatolite from the *Cryptozoan* reef of the Gasconade Formation, St. Francois County, Missouri.

Figure 5-80. Top of a nice stromatolite "head." Cotter Formation, Taney County, Missouri.

Figure 5-81. Digitate stromatolite, Gasconade Dolomite, Lower Ordovician, Laclede County near Lebanon, Missouri.

Figure 5-83. Digitate stromatolite (rockhounds call it red algae) from Spencer County, Winchester, Kentucky.

Figure 5-82. Mozarkite stromatolite. The state rock of Missouri is a pink to purple form of flint or chert known as mozarkite, a conjunction of the words Missouri and Ozarks; it has nothing to do with the Austrian composer.

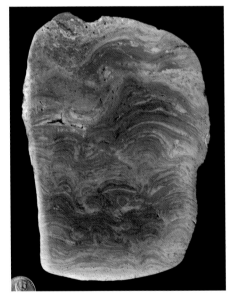

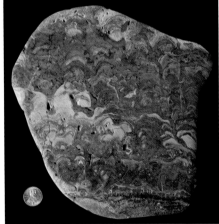

Figure 5-85. Digitate stromatolite in oxidized dolomite. Oneota Formation, Lowermost Ordovician, Tomah, Wisconsin.

Figure 5-84. Lower Ordovician "strom." Oneota Formation. Buffalo County, Wisconsin. Stromatolites are abundant in Lower Ordovician strata of the Upper Mississippi Valley and are similar to those found in the Ozarks.

Figure 5-86. Nice specimen of domal stromatolite, Lower Ordovician, Monroe County near Wilton, Wisconsin.

Figure 5-87. Stromatolite in unoxidized dolomite, Oneota Formation, Appleton, Wisconsin.

Figure 5-88. Manganese oxide-rich stromatolite. Oneota Formation, Oconto County, Wisconsin.

Figure 5-89. *Cryptozoon* sp. (microdomal form). Oneota Formation, Monroe County, Wisconsin.

Figure 5-90. *Conophyton* sp. Horizontal section. Oneota Formation, Oconto County, Wisconsin.

Silurian Period—444 to 420 million years ago

Figure 5-91. Silurian. Plant life has not developed on land at this time. However, some small primitive plants have established themselves along coastal shallow waters and nearshore regions. Some of these primitive plants such as *Cooksonia* and a kind of club moss, *Baragwanathia longifolia*, have been washed to the tidal flood plain. *Eurypterus remipes*, a small sea scorpion, have made their way out of the water during an exploratory foray.

Figure 5-92. Domal "strom" in dolomite. Middle Silurian, Niagarian Stage, Burnt Bluff Formation, Door County, Wisconsin.

Figure 5-94. Laminar stromatolite, Greenfield Dolomite, Huntsville, Ohio.

Figure 5-93. Flip side of the specimen in previous photo.

Figure 5-95. Anomalous "stroms," Prince of Wales Island, Alaska.

Figure 5-96. Oncolitic stromatolite showing distinct laminations from Wood County, Ohio, Salina Formation, Upper Silurian.

Devonian Period—419 to 360 million years ago

Figure 5-97. Devonian. Stromatolites reflect the glow from a red sun as *Goniatites* sp., maneuver in the tidal water. These shelled cephalopods originated from the more primitive Nautiloid*s* during the Middle Devonian some 390 million years ago. Generally the Goniatites are in the deeper saline seas, but here they must have been swept to this shallow by a seasonally strong rising tide. Goniatites may have been opportunistic feeders scavenging on dead animal and vegetative matter, or hunting their prey such as the nearby immature *Cheirolepis* fish. A young *Pterygotus* eurypterid also lingers in this near shore zone.

Figure 5-98. *Girvanella* sp. Lower Devonian oncolites, Attiken Pass, Brooks Range, Alaska.

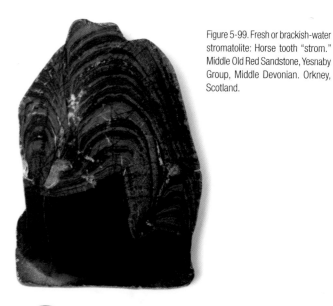

Figure 5-99. Fresh or brackish-water stromatolite: Horse tooth "strom." Middle Old Red Sandstone, Yesnaby Group, Middle Devonian. Orkney, Scotland.

Figure 5-100. Broad domal stromatolite. Lower Devonian, Snowden Mountain, Livengood, Alaska.

Figure 5-101. *Pycnostroma* sp. Middle Devonian, Moscow Formation, Alden, New York.

Figure 5-102. Stromatolite. Hay River, South of Enterprise, Northwest Territories, Canada.

Figure 5-103. Laminar stromatolite replaced with chrysocolla and malachite. Close viewing shows its copper-stained stromatolitic (algal) limestone appearance. Devonian Escabrosa Formation with Jurassic mineralization, Bisbee, Arizona.

Figure 5-104. Oncolitic stromatolite with *Favosites* sp. coral and stromatoporoids. Cedar Valley Formation, Coralville, Iowa.

Carboniferous Period—359 to 300 million years ago

Figure 5-106. *Somphospongia* sp. Surface of a possible hot spring or bacterial stromatolite. Pennsylvanian, Eagle County, Colorado.

Figure 5-105. Carboniferous. During a heavy rain and flood event, *Lepidodendron* logs, a tree that could grow up to 135 feet high, and portions of *Calamites*, a tree-like horsetail, have been washed onto the tidal area of this stromatolite community. Dragonflies with two-foot wingspan take rest in this scene. *Discoserra* fish are seen swimming in the shallow water.

Figure 5-107. *Somphospongia* sp. Possible hot spring stromatolite. Burlingame Limestone, Jackson County, Kansas.

Permian Period—299 to 253 million years ago

Figure 5-108. Permian. A group of *Dimetrodons* are seen in the background milling around in the shoreline vegetation. By the end of the Permian extinction, the *Dimetrodons* will no longer exist. However, the growth of these stromatolitic mats that formed the Lykins formation along east slope of the front range of the Rocky Mountains in northeastern Colorado will continue to lay down their stromatolitic existence into the lower Triassic. These formations may have covered several thousand square miles of the shallow sea during the late Permian.

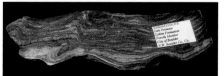

Figure 5-109. Red bed laminar stromatolitic beds. Lyons, Colorado. Red sedimentary rocks (red beds) are especially characteristic of the Permian Period worldwide.

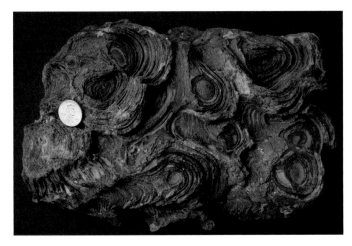

Figure 5-110. Weathered surface of clustered Phosphoria Formation stromatolites from north of Shell, Wyoming.

Figure 5-111. Sliced and polished surface of the previously shown specimen from north of Shell, Wyoming.

Figure 5-112. Tranverse section of naturally weathered surface of *Greysonia*-like stromatolite from the Phosphoria Formation, Big Horn Mountains, near Shell, Wyoming.

Figure 5-113. *Conophyton* stromatolite that appears to have formed on *Stratifera*, upper part of Buckley Formation, Central Transantarctic Mountains, Queen Alexandra Range, Antarctica. *The Polar Rock Repository, sponsored by the National Science Foundation Office of Polar Programs, provided access to this specimen for photographing by Michael Riesch, Earth Haven Museum*

Figure 5-114. Uncut side of previous Antarctic stromatolite. *The Polar Rock Repository, sponsored by the National Science Foundation Office of Polar Programs, provided access to this specimen for photographing by Michael Riesch, Earth Haven Museum*

Mesozoic Era—252 to 67 million years ago

Figure 5-115. Mesozoic. During low tide, a three-foot-tall *Ornitholestes therapod* dinosaur has ventured from the nearby forested area and found its way on top of an exposed stromatolite. Generally the *Ornitholestes* feed on insects, frogs, lizards, and small prey. Today it has collected one of several stranded cephalopod ammonites from the tidal flat. It appears as though the *Ornitholestes* faces a dilemma of whether to drop the ammonite and try to capture the *Dimorphodon* flying reptile feeding on a dead fish.

5-117. Polished cabochon-like slab of Cotham Marble, which has been widely distributed through mineral, rock and fossil shows in Tucson, Arizona; and Munich, Germany.

Figure 5-116. Cotham "Marble." From stromatolite bearing beds of the Late Triassic of southwestern England. These have been cut and polished since the nineteenth century and are known as Cotham "Marble."

Figure 5-118. Freshwater stromatolite, Morrison Formation, Upper Jurassic. A section through a stromatolite from one of the lakes that also harbored dinosaurs. From the dinosaur-rich Morrison Formation near Grand Junction, Colorado.

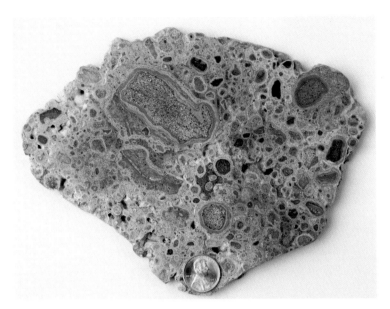

Figure 5-119. Oncolites. Cretaceous from near Denham, Shark Bay Shire (county), Western Australia. Note the algal crust coating clasts. These are probably of freshwater origin.

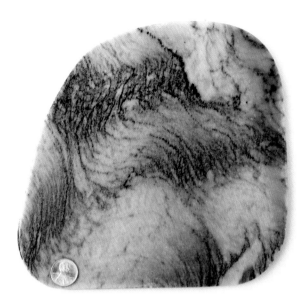

Figure 5-120. Microbial mat from deep-sea environment, Cretaceous, Cycades Formation, Evia Island, Karystes, Greece.

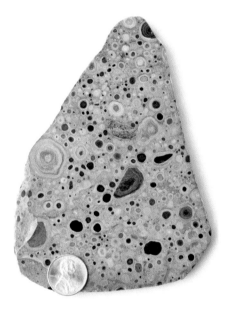

Figure 5-121. Oncolitic stromatolite, Mullarbor Limestone, Miocene, Perth, Western Australia.

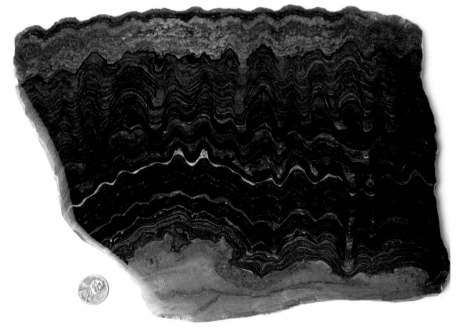

Figure 5-123. Freshwater stroms, Bolivia. These stromatolites have been widely distributed through the Tucson and other fossil shows. Reliable sources (Mindat.org) give them as Cretaceous in age; other sources give Paleozoic as the age. They are almost certainly Phanerozoic in age, but they generally have been mislabeled as being of Precambrian age. Miraflores Formation (stromatolite beds), El Molino, Cerro Huanaquino Potosi Dept, Bolivia.

Figure 5-122. *Microcodium* sp. Oncolitic stromatolite, Narihme Alps, Switzerland.

Cenozoic Era—66 million years ago to present

Figure 5-124. Cenozoic. A September 2012 backcountry field trip to northwest Colorado found the "Ducey" stromatolites illustrated in this painting. These stromatolites measured up to twenty-five feet in diameter. Some of the stromatolites at this site most likely developed in an inland lake and were formed by giant algal heads around silicified rotted tree stumps. Perhaps fish and turtles swam among these living algal communities.

Figure 5-125. Oncolitic stromatolite, Carnarvon, Western Australia. These are similar to Cretaceous forms from the same general area.

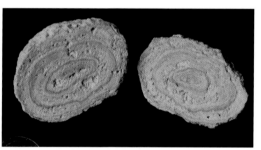

Figure 5-126. Algal concretion (oncolite) from the Paleocene of Montchenot, Ardennes, France.

Figure 5-127. Approximately 37 m.y. old freshwater stromatolite, Owl Butte County, northeast of Newell, South Dakota.

Figure 5-128. *Chlorellopsis* sp. Green River Formation near Maybell, Colorado.

Figure 5-129. Irregular stromatolite, Green River Formation, Lake Gosiute sediments, Wamsutter, Wyoming. A wide variety of stromatolites occur in the Green River Formation of Wyoming, Colorado, and Utah. These are more extensively covered in chapter 8.

Figure 5-130. Small digitate stroms. Green River Formation, Wamsutter, Wyoming.

Figure 5-131. Two halves of a copper-impregnated stromatolite. Green River Shale, Sweetwater Basin, Wyoming, Middle Eocene.

Figure 5-132. *Chlorellopsis* sp. The most widely distributed and best known stromatolite from the Green River Formation, Wamsutter, Wyoming.

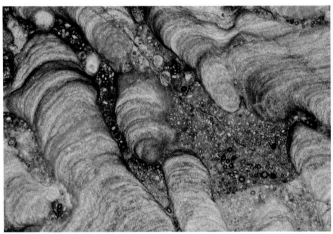

Figure 5-133. *Chlorellopsis* sp. Close-up of this Green River stromatolite shows granules between stromatolite "fingers" that are actually ostracodes (small shelled crustaceans).

Figure 5-134. *Oncholites* sp., Miocene, New Zealand (South Island). Possibly formed on a large lake similar to that which formed the stromatolites of the Eocene Green River Formation of Wyoming.

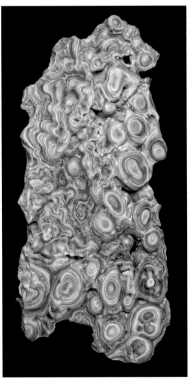

Figure 5-135. A beautiful photo of a 2"×4.5" piece of a freshwater stromatolite from Svoge, Bulgaria. Miocene in age. Parts of this specimen look oncolitic because the stromatolite digits were cut horizontally.

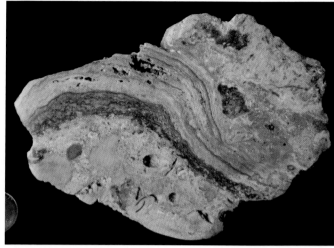

Figure 5-136. Freshwater "strom." Ogallah Formation, Pliocene. Southwest of Clear Lake, western Oklahoma. This may be caliche rather than a bona fide stromatolite; they can look very similar.

Figure 5-137. Stromatolite Miami Oolite, Pleistocene, Homestead, Florida.

Figure 5-138. Pleistocene to modern stromatolite. Marian Lake, Stenhouse Bay, Australia.

Figure 5-139. Uncut domal "strom" (left) and sliced specimen (right). Marion Lake, Stenhouse Bay, Western Australia.

Bibliography

Fenton, Carroll L. and Mildred A. Fenton. 1958. *The Fossil Book*. New York: Doubleday.

Stinchcomb, Bruce L. 1976. "Precambrian algal stromatolites and stromatolitic limestones in the St. Francois Mountains of Southeast Missouri," pp. 122–131. In *Studies in Precambrian Geology of Missouri with a guidebook to parts of the St. Francois Mountains. Contribution to Precambrian Geology No. 6*. Missouri Dept. of Natural Resources, Division of Geology and Land Survey, Rolla, Missouri.

White, Mary E. 2003. *Earth Alive! From Microbes to a Living Planet*. Singapore: Kyodo Printing Co. Pte, Ltd.

Chapter Six

Foolers, Dubiofossils, and Pseudostromatolites

B. L. Stinchcomb

Pseudofossils

Until the 1960s, some paleontologists still questioned the biogenicity of stromatolites—that is, some still questioned whether they really were fossils. This skepticism arose because stromatolites occur in such ancient Precambrian strata, and there was doubt about life having existed that far back in geologic time. Another reason was that stromatolites can resemble geologic phenomena that are undoubtedly inorganic in origin, some of which is shown here. Structures, which look like fossils but are not, are known as pseudofossils (false-fossils); some of them can be real foolers! Indeed many

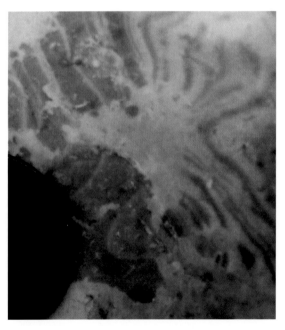

Figure 6-1. "Deer head." Color variations in flint produce something resembling a deer head and neck. Examination of a large number of rocks sooner or later will turn up one that resembles some type of animal or object. For many years, distinguishing between what really is a fossil and what is not was hampered by the common occurrence of pseudofossils like this. Only in the late eighteenth century did scientists universally begin accepting fossils for what they are—the preserved structural evidence of life from the geologic past.

Figure 6-2. "Petrified hamburger." Pseudofossils can come in odd and different shapes. Concretions have been mistaken for bona fide fossils for centuries. They also have been confused with stromatolites. The Ozarks of Missouri and Arkansas are famous for these objects, which were frequently highlighted in St. Louis newspapers under "Our Own Oddities."

such structures have been found in the rock record since the late 1700s when science universally recognized that fossils really were what they are, the evidence of ancient life. Pseudofossils are structures that, like true fossils, exhibit a complex pattern and occur repeatedly in strata, but for various reasons are determined not to be of biogenic origin.

Figure 6-3. The pebble on the right has a hole in it—it's not a fossil. The two pebbles at the left are fossils—pieces of a crinoid stem, a common fossil in the Midwest. Distinguishing between what is and is not a fossil sometimes requires knowledge acquired only through field collecting.

Figure 6-4. "Snail." This is not a fossil; it's a concretion, a rock formed from a chemical nucleation process. Concretions can take on many odd shapes, some resembling animals.

Figure 6-5. Chrysanthemum stone. These radiating crystals resemble fossils—knowledge of the particular strata from which the object was collected may be necessary in determining if the object is or is not biogenic—this one is not!

Figure 6-6. Radiating crystals. These radiating crystals (acicular crystals) might be confused with fossil sponge spicules, which they are not!

Figure 6-7. "Fossil jellyfish." A pressure-related structure in shale associated with a concretion. Such objects have sometimes been considered as fossil jellyfish, especially in the older paleontological literature.

Figure 6-10. Lithophysae. The small spheres that make up much of this slab were formed from a crystallization process occurring in igneous rock. They often are mistaken for fossils.

Figure 6-8. "Czarina." A find associated with puzzling geologic conditions. One of the authors (Stinchcomb) was fooled by this pseudofossil into thinking (for a time) that it might be a late Precambrian vendozoan or a fossil lichen. It's a pseudofossil formed from the puzzling and murky chemistry that forms chert.

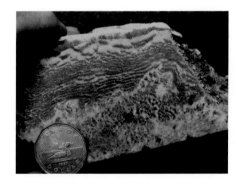

Figure 6-9. *Eozoön canadense*—"the dawn animal of Canada." This pseudofossil (a product of high-grade metamorphism) fooled many late-nineteenth-century geologists who considered *Eozoön* to be the earliest evidence of life.

Figure 6-11. Precambrian "brachiopods." The puzzling objects scattered over this slab resemble poorly preserved, inarticulate brachiopods. They were considered as such by the late-nineteenth/early-twentieth-century paleontologist Charles D. Walcott (1850–1927). They are not primitive brachiopods but probably are biogenic, thus they are dubiofossils, possibly of an unknown (and puzzling) algal life form.

Dubiofossils

Another category of geologic objects that can be confused with stromatolites are known as dubiofossils. Dubiofossils fall between undoubted fossils (like trilobites and dinosaur bones) and pseudofossils, as it is unclear if the object of interest is a fossil. Until the mid 1960s, stromatolites were often considered dubiofossils: some geologists and paleontologists considered them to be true fossils (and hence organic) while others considered them to be pseudofossils (and thus inorganic). The finding of well-preserved microfossils in the ancient Gunflint Chert of Canada, discussed elsewhere, essentially changed this. By the end of the 1960s, stromatolites (for the most part) became universally accepted by most earth scientists to be what they are—structures produced by the life activities of groups or colonies of microscopic life. Thus, stromatolites are now considered to be true fossils that fall under the category of trace fossils, or what has also been called technical fossils. Even today, however, some paleontologists still question Archean stromatolites biogenicity. The authors consider that all of the Archean stromatolites they have seen to be true stromatolites and thus that microbial life on Earth is a very ancient phenomena.

Figure 6-12. *Carelozoon*? Sac-like structures from Finland made of graphite have been given the form genus *Carelozoon*. These flattened forms from the Grenville Marble of Quebec are similar. They probably are biogenic in origin, but then again maybe not—they are dubiofossils.

Figure 6-13. Side view showing flattened graphitic spheres of this Grenville Marble dubiofossil.

Figure 6-14. Stromatolite? These structures from Mississippian age limestone (Salem Formation) can be associated with undoubted stromatolites. What is shown here is composed of aragonite and suggests cave speleothems. When they formed, they may have had a biogenic component in their origin and hence could be considered as a type of stromatolite—this however, is not clear. The object is a dubiofossil—it could also be referred to as a dubiostromatolite.

Figure 6-15. Mottled moneran mat? This dubiofossil came through the Tucson fossil show from Australia in 2004. They were sold along with bona fide stromatolites. Identical structures occur in 1.5 b.y. old bedded tuffs in Missouri, which the author has referred to as mottled moneran mats. They may have originated from redox reactions that developed from moneran mats that formed on volcanic tuff deposited in a shallow body of water like a lake.

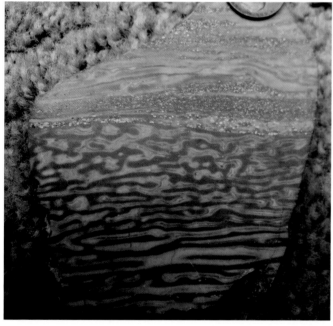

Figure 6-17. The same mottled patterns of possible moneran-mat in a different tuff layer, Mesoproterozoic, Reynolds County, Missouri.

Figure 6-16. This is from 1.5 b.y. old tuffs in Reynolds County, Missouri, possible mottled moneran mat. They may be from redox reactions associated with moneran mats formed on the surface of volcanic ash layers deposited in a shallow body of water.

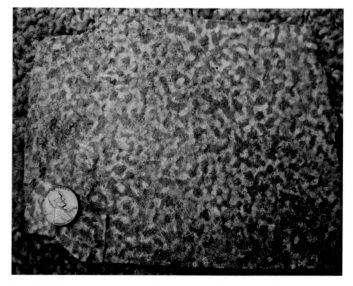

Figure 6-18. The above specimens are side views of these dubiofossil, mottled moneran mats. This is a horizontal slice (top view), same specimen, different view, Reynolds County, Missouri.

Figure 6-19. Mottled moneran mat with beginnings of small domes suggesting a link with small stromatolites[?] Reynolds County, Missouri.

Figure 6-20. Another of these peculiar dubiofossils, Reynolds County, Missouri.

Figure 6-21. Precambrian "caterpillar." What looks like a segmented fossil worm is actually a clast (fragment) in volcanic tuff. The segmented pattern in the clast may, however, be microbial related and hence allied with stromatolites. In the early Precambrian such regular layering of sediment is a characteristic of some stromatolites, as can be seen with the Early Archean Strelley pool "stroms" as well as with Walcott's form genus *Newlandia*. This clast is (possibly) a fragment from such a stromatolite, hence this would make it a dubiofossil.

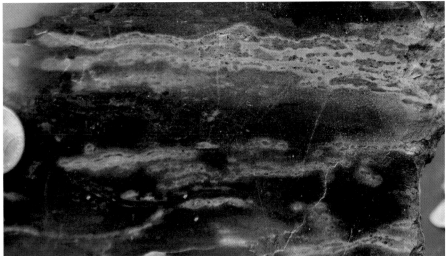

Figure 6-22. Small stromatolites(?) replaced with green epidote. Mesoproterozoic (1.5 b.y. old) bedded tuff (volcanic ash rock) in southern Missouri contain small domal structures like these; they might be metamorphosed stromatolites. Undoubted stromatolites somewhat similar to these and known as *Ozarkcollenia* sp. are found in similar age tuffs in Iron County east of Reynolds County.

Figure 6-23. Outcrop of bedded volcanic tuff along the East Fork of Black River at Johnson's Shut-Ins State Park. The white layers may originally have been thin limestone beds converted to epidote by metamorphism. Epidote replaced stromatolites[?] shown in the previous photo are found just west of here in the same tuff beds and may have had their original calcium carbonate replaced with epidote.

Figure 6-24. Dubiostromatolite. What appear to be laminar stromatolites occur in what has been mapped as Mesoproterozoic rhyolite in the Missouri Ozarks. A better explanation is that it represents silicified biofilm layers formed from microbial growth of either photosynthetic or chemosynthetic bacteria— chemosynthetic monerans either utilizing chemical energy derived from nearby underwater geothermal activity or photosynthetic bacteria utilizing light transmitted through a fairly deep water column. These dubiostromatolite layers, interbedded with either ash flow or bedded tuffs, occur sporadically in the Precambrian (St. Francois Mountains) area of the Missouri Ozarks. They all exhibit variations of the MISS texture discussed in chapter 2.

Figure 6-26. Azurite "suns." These copper carbonate disks from Australia might have a biogenic origin. They occur in sedimentary rock along bedding planes and have consistent shapes. Their odd composition suggests that they might be a type of stromatolite produced by chemoautotrophic monerans. They may have formed from chemosynthetic bacterial physiology that oxidized cupriferous copper to cupric, utilizing chemical energy available from a change in oxidation states of copper ions. The "suns" occur in beds of white kaolinite of either Cambrian or late Precambrian (Neoproterozoic) age.

Figure 6-25. Dubiostromatolite. Similar to the Missouri dubiostromatolites of the previous photo, this also appears to represent biofilm deposits from either photosynthetic or chemosynthetic monerans, possibly associated with igneous and/or geothermal activity. Their geologic age is uncertain where they occur in the Klamath Mountains near the border of California and Oregon. The Klamath Mountains are a geologically complex region partially made up of displaced terrain, possibly from Asia. *Specimen provided by the courtesy of Kathy Dean of Williams, Oregon*

Figure 6-27. "Malachite stromatolites[?]" Massive malachite from the Congo frequently shows patterns that resemble stromatolites. Some could be a type of stromatolite in that they might have had a biogenic origin and be made by copper-oxidizing chemoautotrophs. Some fossil dealers have sold them as such. They might be called dubiostromatolites!

Pseudostromatolites

These are structures that look like stromatolites but are not! Stromatolites must occur in sedimentary rock and have layered deposits consistent with being biogenic. Pseudostromatolites include a variety of structures in the rock record that resemble a stromatolite, but for various reasons—like occurring in igneous rock—are not. Examined as an isolated specimen in a hand sample, many of these look organic, but unless these are observed in their geologic context in an outcrop, they can be real foolers. Various types of concretions found in sedimentary rocks fall into this category, along with accreted structures like speleothems and other secondary calcareous and siliceous objects. A number of structures found in igneous rocks, such as the lithophysae shown here, are also easily confused with stromatolites. This category also includes some phenomena produced as a consequence of high pressure and deep burial and found in metamorphic rocks. The famous Eozoön canadense (the dawn animal of Canada) is an example. Found in highly metamorphosed rock (the Precambrian Grenville Marble), Eozoön was considered the earliest evidence of life until the beginning of the twentieth century, when its pseudofossil status was clearly established. Other phenomena produced as a product of metamorphism have also been considered as early evidence of life and were later proven not to be of biogenic origin.

Figure 6-28. Composite of Moroccan "sand stromatolites." Labeled and sold as stromatolites, these objects from Morocco came on to the fossil market in 2008. They do have a resemblance to bona fide stromatolites but are composed predominantly of sand. They could be biogenic where microbial-produced mucus cemented sand grains together to form a coherent structure.

Figure 6-29. Group of what are not (almost certainly) "stroms" from Morocco at a rock show.

Figure 6-31. Close-up of sand "stromatolites," which are almost certainly sandstone concretions.

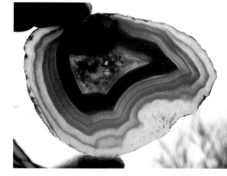

Figure 6-32. Banded agate. The banding of an agate can resemble that of a stromatolite. Subtle signatures characteristic of stromatolites are not present.

Figure 6-30. What have been sold and exhibited as "stroms" are probably groups of sandstone concretions.

Figure 6-33. Lithophysae. Slice-through small spheres produced by crystallization in felsic volcanic tuff. These can suggest oncolites; however, subtle signatures of moneran growth are absent here.

Figure 6-34. Cobble containing numerous grape-sized lithophysae.

Figure 6-35. Some of the bands in lithophysae do mimic (somewhat) those of actual stromatolites.

Figure 6-36. Side view of lithophysae in red, volcanic tuff originally thought by some geologists to be a stromatolite. Differences between those two different geologic structures can be quite subtle.

Figure 6-37. Orange halos surround what are believed to be groups of small lithophysae. These make an interesting and even spectacular pattern, but one quite different from a stromatolite.

Figure 6-38. Slab of greenish rhyolitic tuff from Madagascar. Many polished specimens like this came through the Tucson show labeled and sold as stromatolites (or oncolites). They are attractive but (almost certainly) are not biogenic; they appear to be a type of lithophysae. They also lack some of the subtle signatures of bona fide stromatolites.

Figure 6-40. This is not a stromatolite, although it occurs in stromatolite-bearing strata. It is rather a secondary form of calcium carbonate (aragonite) similar to that which creates cave formations (speleothems). There is some evidence that speleothems owe part of their origin to bacterial activity, so that monerans may have had a hand in their formation. If this were so, they might qualify as dubiostromatolites and thus be classified as a dubiofossil.

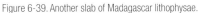

Figure 6-39. Another slab of Madagascar lithophysae.

Figure 6-41. Banding in chert. This is a common pattern found in chert and flint. Although sometimes confused with chertified stromatolites, it lacks the required, often subtle signatures of a true stromatolite. Jefferson County, Missouri.

Figure 6-42. Chert chunk with characteristic non-stromatolite banding. Regular banding like this is secondary and is referred to as Leisegang bands. These are not to be confused with regular microbialite layers, such as those responsible for banding in the Strelley Pool "stroms."

Figure 6-43. Chert with Leisegang bands. This is a variant on chert banding. The bands shown here are quite regular; however, the banding is not a primary structure, as it is on stromatolites. Rather it is secondary, having been formed at some time after the chert formed from the movement of iron oxide through the rock.

Figure 6-44. Sandstone with Leisegang bands (or rings). Formed from slow migration of iron salts through a layer of sandstone, Leisegang bands, when circular like this, can be confused with stromatolites.

Micro-pseudofossils

Pseudofossils occurring at the microscopic level also have been considered fossil micro-organisms, especially some of those found in Precambrian rocks where fossils otherwise appear to be absent. Two occurrences of such micro-pseudofossils are especially notable and interesting, as both were found in meteorites. The first of these, reported in the early 1950s, were the "organized elements" found in the Murray Kentucky meteorite (a carbonaceous chondrite). The other was the infamous nannobacteria found in a Martian meteorite and announced in 1996. Both of these occurrences elicited a lot of public and media interest until their non-biogenic origin was verified.

A Final Word!

Even a novice may recognize some pseudofossils as a rock shaped like an animal or other organism, but others require a knowledgeable person to make a correct diagnosis. The case with dubiofossils, however, is not so easily resolved—many really are problematical and puzzling. One of the most thorough and valuable works on dubiofossils is Hans Hofmann's "Precambrian fossils, dubiofossils and problematica in Canada." This is an especially valuable work as Precambrian rocks usually contain more dubiofossils than are found in younger rocks. Canada (a big place) has vast areas of these ancient rocks that over the years have yielded lots of problematic fossil-like objects.

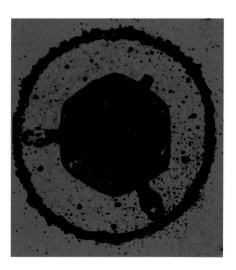

Figure 6-45. Out-of-this-world 1951 micro-pseudofossil. This "organized element" made news in 1951, when examination under high magnification of the recently fallen Murray Kentucky carbonaceous meteorite revealed small objects like this. A number of microscopic structures (crystals) like this were discovered and at the time considered to be possible microfossils. It might be noted that the current rover on Mars has its computer programmed to recognize stromatolite-like shapes and textures as it probes the Martian surface.

Figure 6-46. Martian pseudofossils. When a calcium carbonate-filled cavity in a meteorite found in Antarctic ice (Allen Hills 84001) was examined with an electron microscope, for a time scientists believed it was evidence that primitive life existed on Mars sometime in the geologic past. Like the "organized elements" of the Murray Kentucky meteorite, these objects are now recognized as pseudofossils—they are micro-pseudofossils.

Glossary

Biogenicity. Having an origin through the biosphere and being associated with life: in other words, having once been living or being involved with part of a living organism.

Brachiopod. A phylum of shelled, worm-like organisms that have left an extensive fossil record.

Clast. A rock fragment, pebble, or cobble that now is a component of an outcrop, rock, or other geologic material.

Concretion. A globular mass formed by some sort of nucleation process and generally associated with sedimentary rock. In Phanerozoic rocks, concretions sometimes have a fossil acting as the concretion's nucleus.

Dubiofossil. An object that looks biogenic in origin (like a fossil) but whose origin is unclear; it may or may not be a fossil. Dubiofossils are prevalent in the Precambrian, where they seem to have formed from the activities of microbial communities.

Dubiostromatolite. A subclass of dubiofossil. Dubiostromatolites look like stromatolites, but for various reasons their biogenicity is questioned.

Leisegang bands or rings. Regular bands or rings, usually composed of iron oxide and formed from migration of minerals (especially iron minerals) through porous rock.

Lithophysae (lith-o-fi-se). Sometimes known as "rock bubbles," lithophysae are formed from a nucleation process in felsic (quartz rich) igneous rock, especially rhyolite and rhyolitic tuff, shortly after they formed. They really can look like bona fide fossils.

Organic. Produced by living things, and thus biogenic in origin. In chemistry, however, the word organic can refer to chemical compounds containing carbon and hydrogen even though no biogenicity was involved. This is exemplified in the organic compounds found in meteorites known as carbonaceous chondrites.

Phanerozoic. The period of geologic time in which the fossil record is relatively clear and well-documented. This starts with the Cambrian Period of the Paleozoic Era and includes the Paleozoic, Mesozoic, and Cenozoic Eras of geologic time.

Redox phenomena. Phenomena having to do with chemical reduction and oxidation. Redox phenomena in sedimentary rock can be responsible for regular and repeating patterns produced by a periodic presence of microbial life, and thus a possible biogenic origin for some types of dubiofossils referred to here as "mottled-moneran-mats."

Speleothems. Structures found in caves and formed by dripping water or other processes. Speleothems include stalactites, stalagmites, cave pearls, and other structures that superficially can resemble stromatolites. A microbially induced origin has been suggested for some types of speleothems.

Vendozoans or Edicarin organisms. Organisms of puzzling affinity found as fossils in strata of the latest Precambrian (650–535 m.y. old). Some paleontologists consider Vendozoans to be the soft-bodied ancestors of Cambrian organisms like trilobites, cnidarians, and echinoderms. Other interpretations are that they are fossils of extinct representatives of evolutionary experiments that predate the Cambrian Period and the Cambrian radiation, or spread of invertebrate animals.

Bibliography

Gould, Stephen J. 1980. "Bathybius and Eozoon" in *The Panda's Thumb*. New York and London: W. W. Norton.

Hofmann, Hans J. 1971. "Precambrian fossils, pseudofossils and problematica in Canada." *Geological Survey of Canada Bulletin, Vol. 189.*

Stinchcomb, Bruce L. 2005. "Precambrian Stromatolites Replaced with Epidote in a Prebatholithic Sequence of Reynolds Co., Missouri." (abstract). Proceedings of the 2005 Meeting of the Missouri Academy of Science, Geology/Geophysics Section.

Stinchcomb, Bruce L. 2006. "Possible Biogenic Structures in Prebatholithic Tuffs of the Missouri Precambrian." (abstract). Proceedings of the 2006 meeting of the Missouri Academy of Science, Geology/Geophysics Section.

Stinchcomb, Bruce L. 2004. "Lichenlike Dubiofossils from Sandstone Cobbles from the Missouri Ozarks." (abstract) Geological Society of America, North-Central Section, 38 Annual Meeting, St. Louis, MO.

Chapter Seven

Stromatolites and Hot Springs

B. L. Stinchcomb

Thermophiles and Deposits by Thermophilic Monerans

A rich assortment of often peculiar forms of moneran life can be associated with geothermal activity (areas of hot springs). Cyanobacteria can grade into assemblages of algae in the cooler waters of a geothermal area, especially in a spring branch. Where waters in the 160–180 degree F range occur, colonies of orangish or reddish bacteria can live. The archaea (or archeobacteria) can occur in even hotter water, including monerans collectively known as extremophiles. Specifically, heat-loving forms known as thermophiles occur in the deep part of the spring. Thermophiles of the kingdom Archaea have been found in waters with temperatures as high as 260 degrees F that were previously thought to be sterile. The fossil record of thermophilic monerans is unclear, however, especially with the thermophilic archaea.

Figure 7-1. An aerial view of Norris Geyser Basin, Yellowstone National Park, Wyoming. The basin is the hottest, most acidic and active geothermal area in Yellowstone Park. Despite the area's heat and acidity, monerans known as thermophiles flourish in the basin's many hot springs.

Figure 7-2. Close up of reddish-orange cyanobacteria near a hot spring in the Norris Geyser Basin, Yellowstone Park, Wyoming.

Figure 7-3. Grand Prismatic Spring, Yellowstone National Park, Wyoming. The largest hot spring in Yellowstone with temperatures ranging from 145–188°F. In the cooler outflow areas, photosynthetic bacteria form large, beautifully colored mats ranging from green and yellow to orange and red. In the interior of this hot spring, only hyper-thermophiles can survive.

Figure 7-4. Runoff channels from Emerald Pool, Upper Geyser Basin, Yellowstone National Park, Wyoming. The bands of color in the outflow of Emerald Pool are the result of different bacterial communities existing at different water temperatures. Cyanobacteria containing orange and brown pigments thrive in high, narrow temperature ranges. Green photosynthetic bacteria occur at cooler temperatures.

Figure 7-5. Bacterial mats along the hot stream flowing through Waimangu Volcanic Valley, New Zealand. These mats consist of various photosynthetic bacteria and blue-green algae. The blue-green algae intermingle with the orange bacteria of the genus Chloroflexus.

Archaea have a better chance of leaving a fossil record in the form of chemical compounds formed from decomposition of archean cells—such "chemical fingerprints" have been identified in some very ancient rocks. Archeal membranes contain lipids (fats) chemically different from those of other organisms. These lipids degrade to distinct molecular structures that have been identified in some very ancient sedimentary rocks, some of which include stromatolites.

The atmosphere of the young Earth was probably rich in carbon dioxide, ammonia, and methane, and was most likely quite hot. These conditions, while toxic to plants, animals, and fungi, were hospitable to archaea. Rather than their being odd life forms (as they are by today's standards), living archaea probably represent remnants of thriving communities that had worldwide domination in the young Earth.

Figure 7-6. Photo of the hot stream flowing through Waimangu Volcanic Valley, New Zealand, with photosynthetic moneran mats forming from the hot spring seepage coming from Mount Hazard.

Figure 7-7. Geyser near the shore of Lake Rotomahana, Waimangu Volcanic Valley, New Zealand. Surrounding the geyser are mats of photosynthetic bacteria. Within the geothermal geyser vent itself will be found thermophiles that can withstand very high temperatures.

Figure 7-8. White sinter terraces forming from hot springs near Frying Pan Lake, Waimangu Volcanic Valley, New Zealand. Minerals such as arsenic, tungsten, and molybdenum combine with photosynthetic moneran mats to form the beautiful orange, brown, green, and yellow terraces seen here.

Figure 7-9. Pilot Knob, Missouri, 1871. The top of this Missouri Mountain is composed of beds of volcanic tuff charged with iron minerals, primarily hematite. Geothermal activity is thought to be responsible for this mineralization. In this case, the iron-rich volcanic tuff at its top may have had a connection with chemoautotrophic monerans. Mesoproterozoic rocks of the Missouri Ozarks are predominantly igneous, so that geothermal activity and associated thermophilic monerans may have occurred frequently. The bands going up the side of Pilot Knob were tramways used to carry the mined iron ore down to the base of the mountain.

Conophyton

In cooler waters, cyanobacteria and algae can grow crusty or limy structures, especially if the water has a high load of dissolved ions. Some of the crusts in modern hot springs have a stromatolite-like structure where the walls of the spring are covered with cyanobacteria. In warmer or deeper waters, distinctive stromatolites known by the form genus *Conophyton* can also occur. *Conophyton* can form from a mix of cyanobacteria and bacteria—its teepee-like morphology is distinct from the domes, mats, and fingers of more conventional stromatolites. In the even deeper recesses of geothermal waters can be found the thermophilic archaea—thermophilic organisms occurring as mats that adhere to the walls of the hottest portion of the spring. Archaea, however, unlike cyanobacteria and some bacteria, usually do not deposit mineral or organic material that might be preserved and recognized as fossils.

Figure 7-10. Probable hot spring (or geyser) deposits, Mesoproterozoic, Fredericktown, Missouri. An arrangement of cut slabs from what is believed to be a 1.5 b.y. old hot spring or geyser vent. The center of the structure was filled with white, sparry calcite. Precambrian rocks in the Missouri Ozarks were formed from extensive volcanic activity. What Stinchcomb recognized as the conduit of a hot spring or geyser was encountered during road construction on Highway 67 near Fredericktown, Missouri. Unfortunately, no portion of this conduit is currently exposed.

Figure 7-11. Iron-oxide pigmented calcite and hematite, possibly the result of deposits formed on the wall of a geothermal vent. Precambrian strata outcropping in the geologic center of the Ozarks is predominantly of volcanic origin. Geothermal phenomena such as hot springs and geysers must have been common, and moneran communities would have been present. Note the iron-rich calcite covering dark rhyolite fragments.

Figure 7-12. Iron-rich radiating (acicular) calcite crystals from possible geothermal vent. Fredericktown, Missouri.

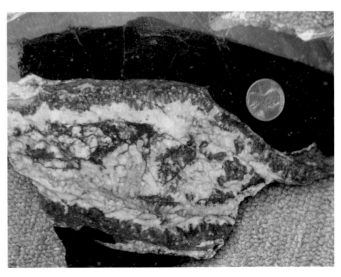

Figure 7-13. Close-up of patterns produced as a (possible) biogenic deposit associated with a geothermal vent—either a hot spring or geyser vent. Mesoproterozoic, Fredericktown, Missouri.

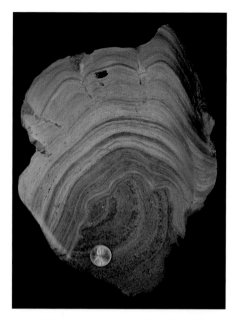

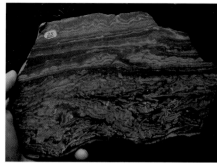

Figure 7-15. *Ozarkcollenia laminata.* This 1.5 b.y. old (alternately designated 1.5 G Y) laminar stromatolite is associated with volcanic tuff in the Missouri Ozarks. The pink color comes from manganese carbonate (rhodochrosite). This distinctive stromatolite might have been associated with geothermal conditions, and the manganese minerals deposited as a result of the physiological activity of chemoautotrophs. Cuthbertson Mountain, Iron County, Missouri.

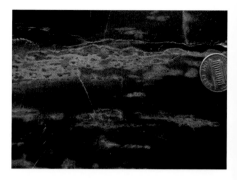

Figure 7-16. Small domal stromatolites? The small epidote domes in this slab of tuff, like those above, may be associated with geothermal activity. The tuff bearing these fragments has been metamorphosed (cooked), converting calcium carbonate to epidote. Reynolds County, Missouri.

Figure 7-14. Freshwater stromatolite, Middle Eocene, Green River Formation, Sweetwater Desert, Wyoming. This stromatolite may have obtained its coloring from minerals during geothermal vent activity.

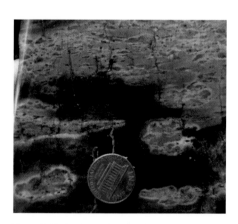

Figure 7-17. Another group of epidote-replaced stroms. Reynolds County, Missouri.

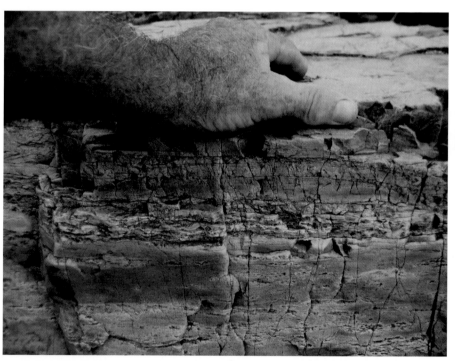

Figure 7-18. Epidote-replaced stromatolite beds (green) in bedded tuff at Johnson's Shut-Ins State Park, Reynolds County, Missouri.

Figure 7-19. Bedded volcanic tuff containing epidote-replaced limestone (thin white layers) of probable cyanobacterial origin. East Fork of Black River, Johnson's Shut-Ins State Park, Reynolds County, Missouri.

Conophyton and Hot Springs

In the hotter waters of a geothermal area, animals cannot live. The biota consist rather of cyanophytes and bacteria forming an ecosystem that almost certainly goes deep into the Precambrian. The cyanobacterial elements appear to be primarily of the genera *Phormidium* and *Chloroflexus*, known for phototaxis and cohesion. Quiet water and the absence of active grazers are likely the

major environmental conditions in forming *Conophyton*. Both conditions exist under geothermal conditions like those found in Yellowstone Park's hot springs, where *Conophyton* can be locally abundant (Brocks et al. 1999). Moreover, Conophyton-like structures have also been grown in the laboratory with pure cultures of the cyanobacteria *Phormidium tenue*.

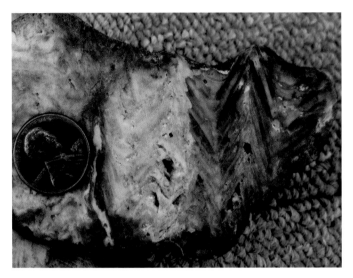

Figure 7-20. *Conophyton* sp. A slice through these distinctive, cone-shaped stromatolites. These specimens of Cambrian age occur (as float) associated with major faults of the Ste. Genevieve Fault Complex, a major geologic feature in the eastern Ozarks of Missouri. Geologists suggest that geothermal activity preceeding movement on the fault may have supported a community of cyanobacteria and thermophilic eubacteria like the genus *Phormidium*, organisms that can produce these cone-shaped stromatolites.

Figure 7-21. Exterior of *Conophyton* mass from near the Ste. Genevieve Fault Complex. The pattern shown here is a variant of that shown in the previous image. It is characteristic of the surface of a *Conophyton* mass.

Figure 7-22. This thinly sliced silicified *Conophyton* has been photographed through transmitted light. The stromatolite fingers are elongate. This material comes from a zone in the 2.3 b.y. old Medicine Bow Mountain sequence near Centennial, Wyoming. *Conophyton* is best known from Precambrian strata—some, like this specimen, are of considerable antiquity. These resemble the vertical trace fossils known as *Scolithos* (or *Scolithus*) that appear at the beginning of the Cambrian Period and are characteristic of Lower Cambrian Sandstones and quartzites. Trace-fossil-like structures, somewhat like *Scolithus*, have been reported from quartzite in the Medicine Bow Mountains, (Kaufmann 1981). They also resemble these specimens of *Conophyton*.

Stromatolite-like Structures Produced by Monerans (Bacteria and Archaea)

Monerans, unlike eukaryotes, can utilize a variety of chemical pathways in their physiology. Whereas photosynthesis is the basic physiologic process supporting most of the earth's biosphere, some prokaryotes, known as chemoautotrophs, have the ability to utilize chemical energy to power their life activities. One of the chemical pathways used for this is the oxidization of metallic ions to a higher valence state. The transition to a higher oxidization state with iron (ferrous to ferric), copper (cupreous to cupric) and manganese (Manganiferous to manganic) are a few examples that provide chemical energy for moneran physiology. It is noteworthy to mention that some stratiform deposits of the above elements (ores) have been attributed to the activities of chemautotrophs that lived in the geologic past. As with the archaea, the fossil record of chemautotrophs is unclear and "muddy."

Bacterial Stromatolites

(Note that bacterial stromatolites are also covered in other parts of this book.)

Bacteria and bacterial stromatolites can be associated with geothermal (hot spring) environments. Like cyanobacteria, some bacteria can photosynthesize, but the photosynthesizing pigment is chemically different (bacteriochlorophyll) from that of cyanobacteria. Cyanobacterial chlorophyll has absorption peaks of red (and infrared), which is different from that of bacteriochlorophyll. This is true also for the blue portion of the spectrum. In stromatolites, photosynthetic bacteria are found in layers occurring underneath the cyanobacterial layers. Rates of photosynthesis between cyanobacteria and photosynthetic bacteria are also considerably different. In modern stromatolites and bacterial mats, these two photosynthetic elements can be distinguished from each other by exposure to carbon dioxide made up of carbon-14 (which is radioactive) and allowing the organisms to photosynthesize, thus incorporating some of the radiocarbon into the organism. A portion of the microbial mat can then be placed in the dark and covered with a liquid photographic emulsion. Allowed to stand for a while, the radioactive carbon in the cells will expose the emulsion. Cyanobacterial cells produce much more emulsion exposure than bacteria cells, indicating that the rate of photosynthesis is considerably greater for cyanobacteria.

Figure 7-23. Non-cyanobacterial stromatolite. The red in this peculiar "strom" from Kansas is iron; the blue may (in part) be from copper. Chemosynthetic bacteria may have had a hand in producing these unique stromatolites from Permian strata near Abilene, Kansas. These "stroms" were once popular with rockhounds. Copper minerals are associated with Permian strata in a number of places around the globe. Its presence in Permian sedimentary rocks, where it sometimes has even been mined, suggests it is microbially related.

Figure 7-24. A broad digitate stromatolite from the Altyn Limestone of the Belt Series of Mesoproterozoic (Middle Proterozoic) age. The main portion of the "strom" is red from hematite formed from the oxidization of ferrous iron from oxygen produced by photosynthetic activity of cyanobacteria. The black layer is probably produced by photosynthetic bacteria, or obligate anaerobes. After awhile they were replaced by the more efficient aerobic cyanobacteria.

Glossary

Archaea. A group of monerans that are genetically distinct from the eubacteria and are considered a separate high-level taxon—the domain archaea. Recent (2013) high-level taxonomy considers three domains of life: the archaea, the bacteria, and the eukaryota, the latter of which includes the kingdoms of animals, plants fungi, protists, and slime molds.

Archeobacteria. The moneran domain archaea.

Bacteria (or eubacteria). The domain of monerans that includes the genetically distinct bacteria and the cyanobacteria. Bacteria are genetically distinct from archaea. Archaea also often occupy ecological niches not occupied by bacteria.

Biota. A group or natural assemblage of monerans. Biota is the equivalent of flora in plants and fauna in the animal kingdom.

Chemoautotrophs. Monerans that utilize a chemical reaction (often oxidization) instead of photosynthesis in their physiology. Some concentrations of heavy metals in the rock record are believed to have been formed by chemoautotrophic bacteria.

Cyanophytes. Another term for cyanobacteria or blue-green algae.

Extremophiles. Monerans (bacteria and archaea) that live under extreme conditions of either high temperatures or salinity.

G. Y. An abbreviation for giga years, which is also a billion years (b.y.). This unit is one used in physics to designate time spans in megatime.

Float. Loose rock on a hillside that "floats" above bedrock from which it was derived.

Halophiles. Monerans that live in high-salinity environments, such as in some parts of the Great Salt Lake in Utah.

Phototaxis. The phenomena of many photosynthetic prokaryotes capable of movement toward a light source. The phenomena is a puzzling one, not totally explained.

Photosynthetic bacteria. Eubacteria associated with buried layers of cyanobacteria that form a substrate below a living cyanobacterial mat. The photosynthetic compound (bacteriochlorophyll) of photosynthetic bacteria is chemically different from chlorophyll and is less efficient in its intake and use of carbon dioxide.

Thermophilic bacteria. Bacteria that can live in the hot water of geothermal regions.

Bibliography

Brocks, Jochen J., Graham A. Logan, Roger Buick and Roger E. Summons. 1999. "Archean molecular fossils and the early rise of Eukaryotes." *Science*, 285:1033-1036.

Kauffman, Erle G., and James R. Steidtmann. 1981. "Are these the Oldest Metazoan Trace Fossils?" *Journal of Paleontology*, 55:923-947.

Knoll, Andrew H. 1999. "A new molecular window on early life." *Science*, 285:1025-1026.

McLaughlin, Dehne and Ray Grant. 2012. "Azurite suns from the Malbunka copper mine Northern Territory Australia." *Rocks & Minerals*, 87:490-501.

Stinchcomb, Bruce L. 2013. "Occurrence of the Stromatolite Conophyton in the Cambrian of Missouri." (abstract). Transactions of the 2013 Missouri Academy of Science Meeting, Geology/Geophysics Section.

Chapter Eight

Stromatolites of Special Beauty and Variety

This chapter contains three sub-chapters. Each part explains and depicts a type of fossilized stromatolite that is prevalent in the fossil market and popular among rockhounds. These stromatolites are striking in their appearance when cut and polished; they are also relatively abundant, which probably accounts for their popularity.

Mary Ellen Jasper
R. J. Leis

I would like to dedicate this part of Chapter 8 to Robert Wiekert, whose name is synonymous with Mary Ellen Jasper.

Bob Wiekert, from Foreston, Minnesota, has devoted the past thirty-five years of his long life to promoting the

beauty and diversity of Mary Ellen Jasper, an amazing stromatolite. At age 57, Bob decided to leave the stress and rigors of owning and running a large cabinet-producing company and devote himself to what he really loves—rockwork with Mary Ellen Jasper. Bob knows the Mesabi iron range

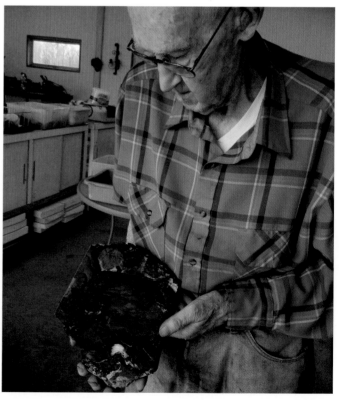

Figure 8-2. Bob Weikert admiring one of his many beautiful slabs of Mary Ellen Jasper. The first time I drove up to Bob's shop and saw his specimens, I told my wife that I thought I had died and gone to heaven.

Figure 8-1. Bob Wiekert with some of his cut and polished slabs of Mary Ellen Jasper. Bob does the cutting and polishing at his shop in Foreston, Minnesota.

Figure 8-3. Bob Weikert standing next to one of the automated polishers he developed, which produces a polish few can duplicate.

Figure 8-4. Bob Weikert cut a thin, transparent slice that, when illuminated from behind, reveals fine details in the stromatolite's digitate "fingers." These fingers are preserved in quartz, unlike most stromatolites, which are made up of calcium carbonate.

as well as anyone and has collected many tons of Mary Ellen over the years. He developed his own automated polishers to obtain a finish unequal anywhere. Bob's knowledge of Mary Ellen is so well regarded that collectors and museums from around the world have enjoyed his strikingly beautiful polished slabs. It was that first beautiful Mary Ellen slab, cut and polished by Bob, that sparked my interest in stromatolites and ultimately led me to write this book. Close-up photos taken from some of his slabs are featured in the book *Ancient Microworlds*, by Giroud Foster and Norman Parker. Bob also prepared an outstanding display of Mary Ellen Jasper housed at the Moose Lake State Park Agate and Geological Center, Moose Lake, Minnesota.

Mary Ellen Jasper is named for the place it was first discovered, the Mary Ellen Iron Mine, St. Louis County, Biwabik, Minnesota. The name Biwabik is the Chippewa word for a piece or fragment of iron. The Biwabik iron formation is part of the Mesabi iron range in northern Minnesota and, along with its correlative, the Gunflint Formation of Canada, is one of the largest iron formations in the world.

Mary Ellen Jasper is the rockhound name for fossil stromatolites found in massive chert beds (the *Collenia undosa* zone of the Biwabik Iron Formation) in the Mesabi Range of northern Minnesota. Stromatolites are a type of trace fossil—structures produced by an organism or group of organisms and preserved in rock over geologic time. These trace fossils are 1.8–1.9 b.y. old. These stromatolites, known as *Collenia undosa* by geologists due to their columnar colonies (digitate stromatolite), occurred in the mid Precambrian and produced oxygen in a shallow marine environment that was rich in ferrous ions (iron in the +2 oxidation state). The combination of ferrous iron and oxygen caused precipitation of the hematite minerals, along with the silica (quartz). Mary Ellen Jasper was formed when iron-rich jasper replaced the algae (cyanobacteria) and

hematite, then filled in around them. It is an example of Superior-type iron formation. Mary Ellen Jasper has a Mohs Scale Hardness of 6.5–7, with red, pink, white, yellow, and green colors. The jasper in Mary Ellen is a type of quartz (silicon dioxide) that is dense and fine grained with 20 percent foreign materials, which determines its color.

In the early days of iron mining in Minnesota, the location of this stromatolite material would indicate that an iron-rich vein was close by. The Mary Ellen stromatolite rock could be as much as fifteen feet thick and would have to be removed before iron mining could commence. To the miners, this material was considered a nuisance and a waste product with no economic value.

In addition to providing us with the iron ore we use every day, iron mining revealed Mary Ellen Jasper to be as beautiful as the finest abstract art. So, thank you, Bob, for sharing your world of Mary Ellen Jasper with us.

These are just a few of Bob's many beautiful specimens. Some of the images are enhanced with close-up photography to show their beauty and abstract appearance.

Figure 8-5. Another dark red slab of Mary Ellen appears to have a somewhat laminar layer sandwiched by digitate "fingers."

Figure 8-6. A red slab of Mary Ellen appears to be brecciated, suggesting that a storm surge broke up the stromatolite.

Figure 8-7. While most Mary Ellen is digitate, this slab appears to be predominantly laminar or wavy.

Figure 8-9. A horizontal slice of green Mary Ellen. When sliced this way, the digitate fingers exhibit concentric rings sometimes referred to as bull's-eye.

Figure 8-8. Green is Mary Ellen's second most common color. It occurs when organic material reduces the iron infiltrating the stromatolite in the ferrous oxidation state. This large museum-grade slab exhibits these beautiful greens.

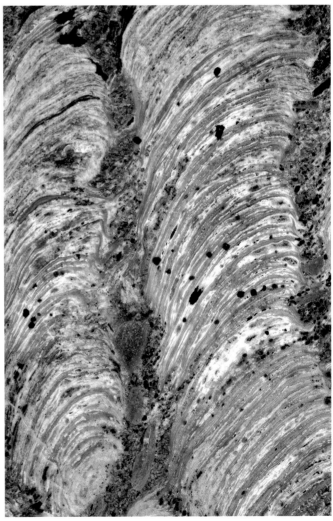

Figure 8-10. Another green Mary Ellen slab with a tinge of red in the digits. The digits appear to be transitioning from green to red.

Figure 8-11. A close-up of figure 8-10 showing the attractive red and green "fingers."

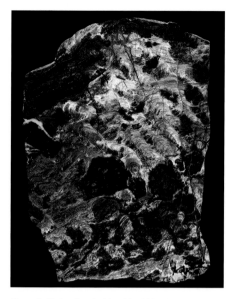

Figure 8-12. A red and white slab of Mary Ellen; the white color is quartz.

Figure 8-14. This brownish slab represents another color in Bob Weikert's Mary Ellen collection. The brown colors occur because the forming stromatolites were impregnated with a slightly hydrated state of ferric iron.

Figure 8-13. A green slab of Mary Ellen exhibiting very long digits. This suggests that Mary Ellen stromatolites formed in very shallow seas.

Figure 8-15. A reddish, brownish, and pink slab of Mary Ellen with black oxidized iron or hematite, with a metallic luster in the middle.

Figure 8-16. A dark red slab of Mary Ellen indicates the presence of a lot of iron oxide in the digits. Red seems to be the most popular color in the fossil market.

Figure 8-17. A gorgeous slab of Mary Ellen exhibiting red, white, and black colored digits. The black digits may be manganese oxide.

Figure 8-18. This yellow Mary Ellen is rare in the fossil market. The yellow colors came about because the ferric iron infiltrating the stromatolite was in a hydrated state (chemically combined with water).

Figure 8-19. This pinkish purple slab of Mary Ellen is another color not often seen in the fossil market. The color is a result of hematite infiltrating the stromatolite in a diluted form indicating small amounts of ferric acid.

Figure 8-20. Close-up of red and white Mary Ellen.

Figure 8-21. Close-up of red and white Mary Ellen.

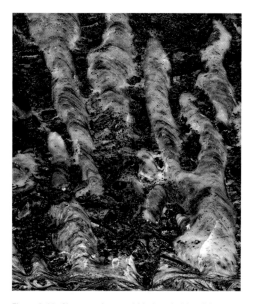

Figure 8-22. Close-up of unusual black and white digitate Mary Ellen.

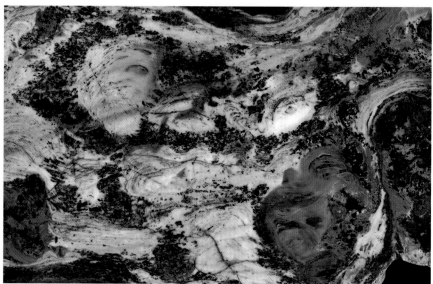

Figure 8-23. Close-up of yellow Mary Ellen.

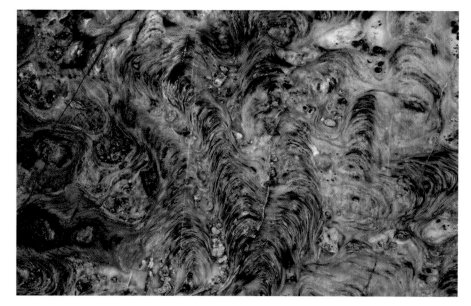

Figure 8-24. Close-up of yellow and green Mary Ellen

Figure 8-25. Mary Ellen Jasper is prized by lapidarists, and here is an example of a beautiful red piece used in a necklace.

Kona Dolomite
R. J. Leis

Kona Dolomite has its own section because of the numerous varieties of this attractive stromatolite-derived rock. Dolomite is a chemical sedimentary rock consisting of the mineral dolomite, a calcium/magnesium carbonate, closely resembling limestone because it probably originated as limestone. Kona Dolomite is not pure dolomite, since silica is also present, and it may include layers of slate, graywacke, and quartzite with gradational phases between these and pure dolomite.

These stromatolitic reefs formed approximately 2.1-2.2 billion years ago in the mid Precambrian. The reefs, which were to become Kona Dolomite, have been subjected to many forces of nature, including intense folding, faulting, and shattering. The Kona Dolomite has been tilted and metamorphosed during multiple geological events. It comes in many shades of red, orange, brown, yellow, pink, and cream; some even have shades of turquoise, brown, gray, and black banding with lacing and mottling. This dolomite gets its colors from trace minerals, mainly iron, and has a Mohs Scale Hardness between 3.5 and 4.

Kona Dolomite is popular with rockhounds and lapidarists because of its varied colors. Its soft texture and colorful appearance appeals to jewelry makers, and its seemingly infinite variety appeals to rockhounds. Kona Dolomite is found in the Kona Hills southwest of Marquette, Michigan, in Marquette County.

If you have an interest in collecting your own Kona Dolomite, there is an opportunity every August, when the Lindberg Quarry in Negaunee, Michigan, gives the Ishpeming Rock and Mineral Club permission to collect in its quarry. Those who attend the August meeting and pay a small fee may collect all the Kona Dolomite they can carry. Illustrated here are some of the many specimens I have obtained over the years. I am sure I don't have all the varieties out there, and that is what makes Kona Dolomite so fascinating.

Figure 8-26. Aerial photo of the large outcrop of Kona Dolomite across from the tourist information center at the junction of Michigan highways 28 and 41, Marquette, Michigan. *Photo courtesy of William Savola*

Figure 8-27. Author R. Leis standing next to an exposed outcrop of Kona Dolomite near the tourist information center, Marquette, Michigan.

Figure 8-28. Another photo of the Kona Dolomite exposure near the Marquette, Michigan, tourist information center.

Figure 8-31. A laminar, iron-rich slab of Kona Dolomite, Chocolay Hills, Marquette County, near Marquette, Michigan. This slab is so iron rich as to be almost banded-iron-like.

Figure 8-32. A unique Chocolay Hills piece of Kona. It is the only piece the collector, Dan Damrow, has ever seen. He notes that the small, tornado-like domal colony, indicated by two arrows, was apparently trying to form in the laminar layers. This is an indication that the zone in which it was formed was changing rapidly.

Figure 8-29. A large block of Kona Dolomite, approximately two feet by three feet and two feet in diameter. It is being used as riprap along the Lake Superior shore, near the Marquette, Michigan, tourist information center.

Figure 8-30. Close-up of the chunk of riprap showing its stromatolite structure.

Figure 8-34. A unique form genre of Kona, Chocolay Hills. On the bottom of this specimen is a laminar stromatolite and the domal bulbous form that emerged on top if it. The domal bulbous form is narrower at the base of the bulb. It is one of two pieces Damrow has seen.

Figure 8-33. A beautiful, unusually colored pink piece of Kona. This material would be prized by lapidarists.

Figure 8-35. Another large slab of domal Kona, Chocolay Hills, Michigan.

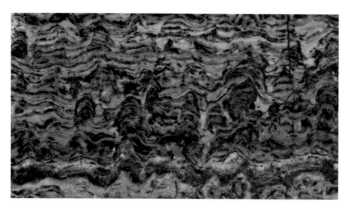

Figure 8-37. A close-up of the previous specimen showing the multi-layered digitates.

Figure 8-36. Here is an example of the rare occurrence of digitate Kona stromatolite found in the Kona mine at Ishpeming, Michigan.

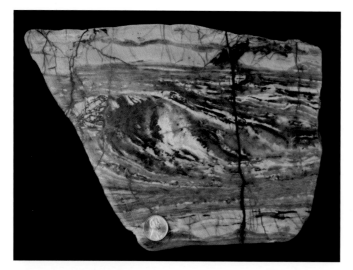

Figure 8-38. An example of ripped and torn laminar Kona, Chocolay Hills, Michigan. The laminar stromatolite has been somewhat rolled up, most likely by a storm surge. This specimen illustrates how shallow the environment was when it was forming, as it appears that waves really tore into it.

Figure 8-39. Another unusual Kona specimen, Chocolay Hills, Michigan. This stromatolite was laminar at one time; a storm came along and pulled up the layers almost in "turkey feather" fashion. This is not domal; it is the intermediate stage between laminar and a free-floating oncolite. The torn layers then became overgrown with laminar stromatolite.

Figure 8-40. A specimen of free-floating oncolitic Kona, Chocolay Hills, Michigan. The nucleus for these oblong oncolites were thin pieces of laminar stromatolite that were ripped up during storm surges.

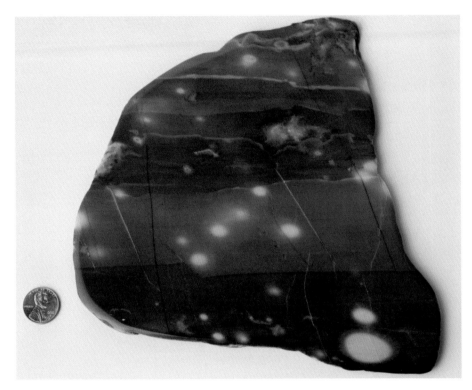

Figure 8-41. A strange piece of laminar Kona, Chocolay Hills, Michigan, with discolored orbs. One speculation is that the orbs of yellow or orange were created by bacterial colonies that may have reduced the iron out of the iron-rich dolomite, thus resulting in the lighter-colored orbs.

Figure 8-42. A laminar piece of Kona, Chocolay Hills, Michigan, that rockhounds sometimes refer to as "lace stromatolite."

Figure 8-43. A slab of laminar Kona, Chocolay Hills, Michigan, that grew in a zone so hyper-saline that selenite crystals developed. As the stromatolite was replaced by dolomite, so were the selenite crystals. This is great evidence of a hyper-saline environment.

Figure 8-44. A laminar piece of Kona, Chocolay Hills, Michigan, clearly exhibiting micro-faulting.

Figure 8-45. A wavy specimen of Kona, Chocolay Hills, sometimes referred to as "butterscotch" by rockhounds. Note the three injection seams in this piece.

Figure 8-46. A large piece of Kona that rockhouds commonly refer to as moose blood. The moose blood term refers to the ½-inch to ¼-inch calcite rhombohedrons that are iron-stained, almost to the color of blood. Some layers have abundant amounts of these crystals.

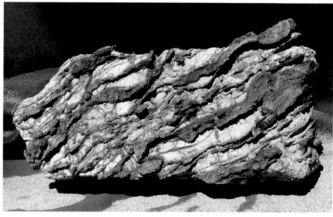

Figure 8-47. A ventifacted piece of Kona, probably deposited by a glacier and then sandblasted by the wind. Found in Marquette County, Marquette, Michigan. *Photo courtesy of William Savola*

Figure 8-48. Kona Dolomite is sought after for its lapidary qualities. I found this ventifacted piece of Kona, collected by William Savola, and this jewelry at Moonstone Gallery in Marquette, Michigan. I put the ventifacted Kona and the Kona jewelry together to capture the final image of this section of the chapter.

Green River Stromatolites
B. L. Stinchcomb

One of the most widely distributed fossil stromatolites are geologically young examples from the Eocene (Early Cenozoic) Green River Formation of the American West. The Green River Formation consists of a series of extensive lacustrine (lake) deposits in Colorado, Wyoming, and Utah. It is best known for its well-preserved and abundant fossil fish. Most of the well-known and widely distributed fossil fish are derived from these sediments.

These sediments, deposited some 45–55 million years ago (just yesterday compared with other stromatolites shown in this book), contain a variety of preserved insects, turtles, amphibians, fish, and plants, sometimes accompanied by stromatolites. Most of the Green River Formation was deposited in three lakes, the smallest of which is Fossil Lake. Green River sediments deposited in Fossil Lake crop out in western Wyoming near the town of Kemmerer. Lake Uinta lies south of Fossil Lake and mostly in Utah. It is here, and in adjacent Colorado, that much of the widely publicized oil shale deposits of the Green River Formation occur. Unlike Fossil Lake, Lake Uinta was very shallow, subsiding slowly as it received sediments from the uplifting Rocky Mountains.

Figure 8-49. Large laminated calcareous Eocene age stromatolite formed by algae mats in the shallow waters of what was once Lake Uinta. This Collenia-type stromatolite may have formed in part by *Chlorellopsis* sp. of green algae. Douglas Pass, Green River Formation, Garfield County, Colorado.

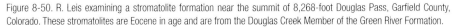

Figure 8-50. R. Leis examining a stromatolite formation near the summit of 8,268-foot Douglas Pass, Garfield County, Colorado. These stromatolites are Eocene in age and are from the Douglas Creek Member of the Green River Formation.

Figure 8-51. Small stromatolites on the surface of a large limestone slab. Lake Uinta portion of the Green River Formation, Douglas Pass, Colorado. This location has also produced fossil insects.

Figure 8-52. The rolling yet rugged landscape of the Green River Formation, whose sediments intermingle with sediments of the Eocene Wasatch Group. Lysite, Wyoming.

Figure 8-53. *Chlorellopsis* sp. This is the most widely distributed and best-known stromatolite from the Green River Formation. *Chlorellopsis* is a digitate stromatolite that appears to have formed from a mix of cyanobacteria and green (eukaryotic) algae. This specimen comes from sediments deposited in the earliest stages of existence of Lake Uinta, during the Paleocene Epoch of the Cenozoic Era. This earliest or Paleocene part of the Green River series of lakes is sometimes known as Lake Flagstaff.

Figure 8-54. Slabby beds of limestone in the Green River Formation near Soldier's Summit, Utah. These were deposited in the shallows of lake Uinta. They often contain the tracks of shore birds that walked on limey "mud" flats during the Eocene Epoch.

Lake Gosiute Sediments and Stromatolites

Stromatolites are common in the sediments of Lake Uinta, but they are not particularly attractive or striking. The third Green River Lake was Lake Gosiute, a large and shallow lake similar to Lake Uinta. Green River Formation sediments of Lake Gosiute are found mainly in Wyoming east and southeast of those of Fossil Lake. Lake Gosiute sediments include those around the southwestern Wyoming town of Green River, the place where the formation originally was named from cuttings made by the first transcontinental railroad in 1869. Sediments deposited at the eastern part of Lake Gosiute contain volcanic ash, which was the source of quartz that has silicified Green River sediments in this area. This silicification produced a variety of agates popular with rockhounds and include what is popularly known as "Turitella agate." The process also produced silicified stromatolites known as "algae agate." These silicified Green River sediments occur on the continental divide, especially in what is known as the continental basin, a relatively flat area crossed by Union Pacific's first trancontinental railroad. Silicified material is especially prevalent south of Wamsutter, Wyoming, where it crops out in sagebrush prairie.

Especially large stromatolites that grew in Lake Gosiute occur in northwestern Colorado, near Maybell. Some of these cap an escarpment formed from dolomitic limestone of the Green River Formation.

Figure 8-55. *Chlorellopsis* sp. Slice through a colony of digitate stromatolites deposited in Lake Gosiute. Green River Formation forming part of the Continental Divided Basin south of Wamsutter, Wyoming.

Figure 8-56. *Chlorellopsis* sp. (large form). These Green River stromatolites come from what is known as the Great Divide Basin, a large, uplifted area of Green River rock deposited in Lake Gosiute and now exposed about ten miles southwest of Wamsutter, Wyoming.

Figure 8-57. Digitate stromatolites of the form genus *Chlorellopsis* sp. It has been suggested that green algae (which is a eukaryote) rather than cyanobacteria (which is a prokaryote) were responsible for many of the Green River stromatolites. Also in many Green River digitate "stroms" like this, ostracode valves fill in between stromatolite fingers, something not seen in earlier stromatolites.

Figure 8-58. Small domal stromatolites. This block was cut from large stromatolitic masses that occur in ravines formed in the Great Divide Basin south of Wamsutter, Wyoming. Like many Precambrian "stroms," these small domes produce a composite to make large domal stromatolite masses that grew either on the edge of Lake Gosiute or miles from the shore, but in shallow water. Occurring interstitially between these large stromatolite masses were vast numbers of the freshwater gastropod (snail) *Oxytrema* sp. Rockhounds know these silicified concentrations of these gastropods as Turritella agate.

Figure 8-59. Turritella agate. Masses of the freshwater snail *Oxytrema* sp. (which occur between stromatolites) have been replaced with quartz (silicified) in Green River sediments deposited in that portion of Lake Gosiute, which now form part of the Continental Divide. Silicification of sediments in other portions of the Green River Formation is not so prevalent as it is south of I-80 near Wamsutter, Wyoming, where these specimens came from.

Figure 8-60. Polished specimens of the freshwater gastropod *Oxytrema* that have weathered from gastropod-rich rock formed in Lake Gosiute and found south of Wamsutter, Wyoming.

Figure 8-61. Coquina made up of the gastropod *Oreoconus* sp. from rock deposited near the eastern edge of Lake Gosiute near Baggs, Wyoming. Like *Oxytrema*, snails can thrive in waters rich in algae, and these snails probably fed on the stromatolites in Lake Gosiute.

Figure 8-62. Pinnacles of Green River sediments near Bonanza, Utah.

Figure 8-63. Vein of gilsonite in the Green River Formation near Bonanza, Utah. The petroleum-bearing beds of the Green River Formation (oil shales) were the source of the petroleum that formed gilsonite (a heavy tar-like residue). Gilsonite is here being mined from a gilsonite filled "crack" in the Green River strata. This gilsonite-filled joint was mined in the 1960s when this picture was taken. The Green River Formation has been prospected extensively for its petroleum-rich beds, but no economical method to extract its petroleum has been forthcoming. Petroleum in the Green River Formation was probably derived from the extensive growth of algae in the three lakes in which the Green River Formation was deposited.

Figure 8-64. Terrain characteristic of the Green River Formation on the Colorado Plateau. These sediments were deposited in Lake Gosiute.

Figure 8-65. R. Leis and illustrator T. McKee standing on the stromatolite-covered surface of what is known as Delaney Rim, a limestone escarpment of the Green River Formation. Delaney Rim forms a spectacular ridge in southwestern Wyoming. The red sediments at the bottom belong to the Wasatch Group, which is also of Eocene Age.

Figure 8-66. T. McKee examining stromatolite fragments littering the surface of Delaney Rim in southwestern Wyoming; red, clay-rich Wasatch sediments are visible below the ridge.

Figure 8-67. Typical "burly" stromatolite from the previously shown locality on Delaney Rim, Wyoming.

Figure 8-68. "Burly" Delaney Rim stromatolites partially covered with orange lichens.

Figure 8-69. Close-up of Delaney Rim "burly" stromatolites.

Figure 8-70. Oncolite. Fossil snail covered with algal layers to produce an oncolite. Oncolites can form around a pebble, a stromatolite fragment, or any object that provides a surface on which algal filaments become attached. Oncolites with a gastropod as a nucleus like this are common fossils on parts of the Delaney Rim.

Figure 8-71. Fossil Butte formed from sediments deposited in Fossil Lake, the most western of Green River Formation outcrops. Fossil Lake sediments are the source of most of the fossil fish seen on the fossil market and quarried from the soft limestone found here.

Figure 8-72. Slabby beds of limey shale in the Green River Formation at Fossil Butte. These sediments were deposited in the most western of the three Eocene lakes.

Figure 8-73. Fossil-bearing shale of Fossil Butte taken before the area was made into Fossil Fish National Monument.

Figure 8-74. *Knightia eocaena*. The most common fossil fish in the Fossil Lake deposits of the Green River Formation. Literally tens of thousands of specimens have been collected from pits near Kemmerer, Wyoming.

Figure 8-75. *Phareodus testis* Cope. Less common in the fossil lake deposits than *Knightia*, *Phareodus* was a carnivorous fish. Carnivorous animals, occupying a higher trophic level in food chains, are generally less abundant than herbivorous fish.

Figure 8-76. *Prisicara serrata* Cope. Another widely distributed fossil fish from Fossil Lake sediments of the Green River Formation.

Figure 8-77. *Gosiutichthys parvus*. Laney Member, Green River Formation. Part of a mass mortality slab of these small fishes, the most common fossil fish in the Lake Gosiute sediments of the Green River Formation.

Figure 8-78. Typical Green River terrain, northwest Colorado, Moffat County, near Maybell, Colorado.

Figure 8-79. R. Leis and T. McKee on outcrop of dolomitic limestone in the Green River Formation deposited in eastern Lake Gosiute, near Maybell, Colorado.

Figure 8-80. R. Leis and T. McKee near a large Green River stromatolite at the left, near Maybell, Colorado.

Figure 8-81. More large stromatolites made up of dolomitic limestone. Moffat County, near Maybell, Colorado.

Figure 8-82. R. Leis looking at large "stroms" covering hills near Maybell, Colorado.

Figure 8-83. R. Leis and Linda Leis next to a large stromatolite. Moffat County, near Maybell, Colorado.

Figure 8-84. Stromatolite with a hole created by a tree that grew in shallow Lake Gosiute and became the nucleus of this large specimen near Maybell, Colorado.

Glossary

Breciated. Angular fragments cemented together.

Calcite. A white or colorless mineral consisting of calcium carbonate.

Calcium carbonate. A white, insoluble solid occurring naturally as chalk, limestone, marble, and calcite.

Cryptozoan. Stromatolite morphology that is domal.

Ferric iron. Iron that has lost three electrons and is present in such minerals as hematite and goethite. Ferric iron is relatively insoluble in water.

Ferrous iron. Iron that has lost two electrons and therefore is in a more reduced state than ferric iron. Ferrous iron compounds are usually water-soluble.

Graywacke. A dark, coarse-grained sandstone containing more than 15 percent clay

Hematite. A reddish-black mineral consisting of ferric oxide, an important ore of iron.

Hypersaline. A land-locked body of water that contains significant concentrations of sodium chloride or other mineral salts, with saline levels surpassing that of ocean water.

Iron oxide. Chemical compounds composed of iron and oxygen.

Metamorphosed. The process by which rocks are altered in composition, texture, or internal structure by extreme heat, pressure, and the introduction of new chemical substances.

Manganese oxide. Any of a variety of inorganic compounds made of manganese and oxygen. It may also form mixed oxides with other metals such as iron.

Riprap. A loose stone used to form a foundation for a breakwater or other structure.

Selenite. A form of gypsum occurring as transparent crystals, sometimes in thin plates.

Silica. A hard, unreactive, colorless compound that occurs in the mineral quartz and as a principal constituent of sandstone and other rocks.

Ventifacted. Rocks that have been abraded, pitted, etched, grooved, or polished by wind-driven sand or ice crystals.

Bibliography

Foster, Giraud, and Norman Barker. 2000. *Ancient Microworlds*. San Francisco: Custom & Limited Editions.

Rigby, J. Keith. 1976. *Field Guide: Northern Colorado Plateau*. K/H Geology Field Guide Series. Dubuque, IA: Kendall Hunt.

Chapter Nine

Petrified Wood with Algae and Other Materials of Biogenic Origins

R. J. Leis

This chapter will be devoted to types of fossil materials that are not entirely stromatolitic.

Cenozoic (Geologically Young) Stromatolites and Petrified Wood

One of the stromatolitic/biogenic rocks covered in this chapter is petrified wood containing both fossil algae and stromatolites. I have always admired the beauty and diversity of petrified wood, but never got into collecting more than a piece or two. The petrified wood category is so vast and encompassing that I was somewhat intimidated about

beginning to collect this material. However, when I discovered that some petrified wood is associated with algae and stromatolites, I was hooked. Here was a more manageable type of petrified wood and one that also encompassed my primary stromatolite interest.

I found my first piece of petrified wood with stromatolites at the Arizona Mineral and Fossil Show in Tucson. This material was from the Barstow Formation, San Bernardino County, Barstow, California—it was a tree branch encased

Figure 9-1. The branched, stromatolite-covered petrified wood at the Tucson Gem, Mineral, and Fossil Show that I admired but was already sold.

Figure 9-2. Tree branch with stromatolites, which I added to my collection. Miocene in age, Barstow Formation, San Bernardino County, Barstow, California.

in stromatolites. I fell in love with that branch, but unfortunately it was sold. Later I obtained a slab of this Barstow material for myself.

The next petrified wood material that I fell for was Eden Valley petrified wood from the Green River formation in Wyoming. Eden Valley wood formed from trees that had been growing and were washed into what was a series of large inland lakes approximately 45 million years ago. This wood exhibits features not found in fossil wood anywhere else on the planet. The preservation process involved abundant algae growing in the lakes. For reasons that aren't completely known, the wood existed in these algae-infused lakes in near-live condition. Algae adhered to the surface, creating a mold around it. Later the wood dried out and shrank inside the algae coating. Eventually the algae casts along, with the shrunken wood, were infiltrated with silica and became rock-like. Silica-rich water seeped through the rock, then petrified the wood and filled in the spaces left between the dried wood and the hardened algae coat with agate, a type of quartz. As the algae coated the inside surface, it left perfect impressions of the bark in the agate. Thus, some of this petrified wood shows 45-million-year-old "pictures" of the same tree — one picture of how the plant looked alive and another after it died and dried out. Eden Valley wood is some of the most beautiful anywhere and we can thank the algae for that.

Figure 9-3. A beautiful petrified tree branch encased with algae, Eocene in age, about 45 m.y.a., Green River Formation, Blue Forest, Eden Valley, Wyoming.

Figure 9-4. Fossil limb cast in freshwater stromatolite. Middle Eocene, Green River Formation, Blue Forest, west of Farson, Wyoming. Blue Forest denotes the presence of blue chalcedony, a form of quartz.

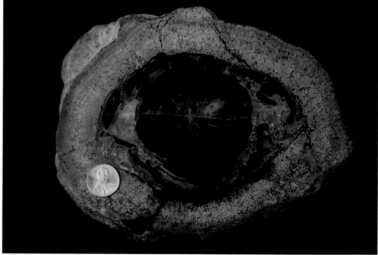

Figure 9-5. Petrified wood limb covered with a thick rind of freshwater stromatolites. Eocene in age from the Green River Formation, Blue Forest, Eden Valley, Wyoming.

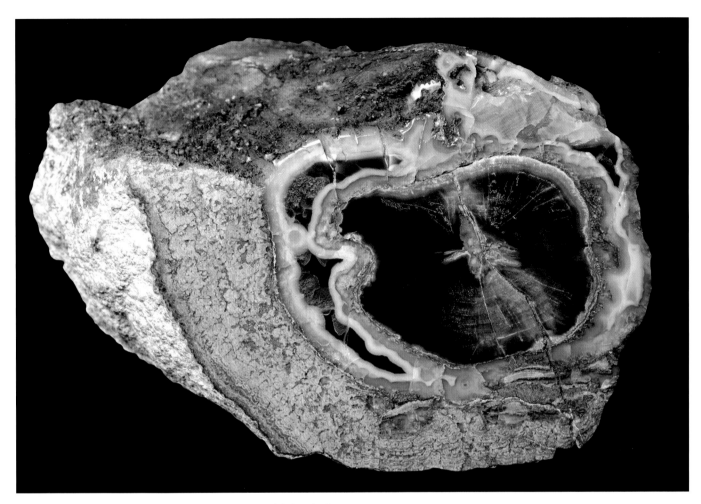

Figure 9-6. A Blue Forest limb, 2.5 × 4 inches, with algae and yellow calcite from the Green River Formation, Eocene, Eden Valley, Wyoming.

Impressive Green River "Stroms"

Another spectacular algae-covered wood can be found in the Ducey stromatolite locality, near Maybell, Colorado. These stromatolites are in the form of concretions, which, like other stromatolites, are the fossilized remains of microbial mats that formed in limestone or dolostone-forming environments. Most of the concretions range in size from three feet in diameter up to ten feet in diameter. The largest can be thirty feet high and twenty feet across. These concretions formed around large algal heads, which themselves formed around a forest of silicified tree stumps. Like Eden Valley wood, these concretions are found in the Green River Formation (the Laney Member) and thus are also Eocene in age.

Figure 9-7. Terry McKee and R. Leis are dwarfed by a gigantic, Eocene-age algal head formed around a silicified tree stump. This formed in freshwater Lake Gosiute, in what is now Moffat County, Ducey stromatolite area, Green River Formation, near Maybell, Colorado.

Figure 9-8. R. Leis and Linda Leis next to another Ducey dolomitic stromatolite-covered tree stump.

Figure 9-9. R. Leis next to a smaller Ducey stromatolite with concentric algae layers that formed around a wood branch nucleus.

McDermitt Oregon Petrified Wood with "Stroms"

Another type of petrified wood with nice stromatolites attached comes from near McDermitt, Oregon, and is Miocene in age. Like the Green River "stroms," these stromatolites also formed in fresh water lakes, attaching themselves to wood that was later replaced by minerals and thus petrified. Petrified wood from Tonopah, Nevada, can be assumed to have formed in a similar manner as the McDermitt wood.

Figure 9-10. Petrified limb in algae thought to be locust, (*Robinia* sp.*)*, Trout Creek Formation, McDermitt, Oregon. Miocene in age.

Figure 9-11. Petrified limb thought to be spruce (*Picea* sp.), encrusted with algae/stromatolites. The rounded stromatolite shapes are very evident in this specimen. From the Trout Creek Formation, McDermitt, Oregon. Miocene in age.

Figure 9-12. An especially pretty petrified wood limb, thought to be yew (*Taxus* sp.) formed in Tertiary Volcanics, Tonopah, Nevada. Stromatolite fingers are clearly visible on this piece of yew.

Figure 9-13. A limb thought to be conifer surrounded by a spectacular display of stromatolite that used the wood as a support for its formation. This specimen is from McDermitt, Oregon, and is Miocene in age.

Oregon Bog Jasper

Oregon Bog Jasper, also known as Gary Green Jasper or Larsonite, is another material that I find to be beautiful and intriguing. This material comes from an area near the Nevada/Oregon border. Bog Jasper is not a stromatolite, but algae is thought to be part of its composition, which makes it eligible for inclusion in this chapter. Bog Jasper is beautiful as a collectible and is often made into jewelry. I first became aware of this material when I found some pieces of it at the Jack Pine Rock Shop in Hayward, Wisconsin. I have subsequently picked up more of this material at the Denver Gem, Mineral, and Fossil show.

Oregon Bog Jasper is essentially petrified swamp material of the prehistoric past (11–14 m.y.a.), consisting of algae, moss, ferns, grass, wood, and mud that accumulated over millions of years. This organic debris was then covered by volcanic ash and eventually became embedded with silica-rich minerals. Bog jasper comes in many shades of green, blue, and earth-tone colors resulting from minerals that seeped into the mixture. The green color comes from ferrous iron minerals found in bog jasper. Some people claim that you can smell decaying vegetation when cutting Oregon Bog Jasper.

Figure 9-14. Piece of Bog Jasper also known as Gary Green, Larsonite, or Oregon Bog Jasper. This specimen comes from Trout Creek Formation, McDermitt, Oregon, and is 11–15 m.y. old. McDermitt is an unincorporated community straddling the Nevada-Oregon border, thus the Nevada label.

LARSONITE
NEVADA

Figure 9-15. A large, beautiful piece of Bog Jasper from the Trout Creek Formation, McDermitt, Oregon, Miocene in age. I obtained this specimen from collector Phil Johnson, Sparks, Nevada. He informed me that two volcanic events helped shape this material—one before the bog material was laid down and one after or on top of it.

Figure 9-16. Bog Jasper specimen from the Trout Creek Formation, McDermitt, Oregon. Phil Johnson had some of this bog material analyzed to learn it's composition. The analysis revealed it to be composed of thirty-six elements, twenty-two of them in trace amounts of 1–52 ppm. The top five elements were iron 46,600 ppm, aluminum 11,000 ppm, potassium 5,030 ppm, sodium 1,550 ppm and calcium 1,020 ppm.

Rhynie Chert

Rhynie Chert is similar to Bog Jasper, found near the village of Rhynie, Aberdeenshire, Scotland, and early Devonian in age. This chert contains exceptionally well-preserved plant, fungus, lichen, and animal material petrified in three dimensions from being embedded in silica from a hot spring. Most of the chert consists of primitive plants along with arthropods, lichens, algae and fungi. The Rhynie chert is scientifically significant because it preserves some of the earth's first land vegetation.

The chert was formed when silica-rich water from geothermal or volcanic springs rose rapidly and petrified this early terrestrial ecosystem. Fossilization occurred as silica from the hot springs flooded the surrounding areas and then permeated into a Devonian peat bog.

This fossil bed is remarkable for two reasons. First, the age of the site (Early Devonian, about 410 m.y.a.) places it at an early stage in the plant colonization of land. Second, these cherts are famous for their exceptional state of preservation, with individual cell walls easily visible in polished specimens.

Bona fide cyanobacteria are preserved in Rhynie chert. The fossils are filamentous, around 3 µm (0.00012 inches) in diameter, and grew on plants and in the sediment itself. They occasionally formed structured colonies, which went on to create microbial mats—the stuff of stromatolites!

Figure 9-17. A mural depicting an Early Devonian (326 m.y.a.) site near what is now known as Rhynie, Scotland. Very early primitive land plants can be seen growing in this ancient scene. This photo was provided by Chase Studios, Cedar Creek, Missouri, and they also constructed the mural.

Figure 9-18. A chunk of Rhynie Chert showing Early Devonian stems or roots of early fossil land plants, from Rhynie, Aberdeenshire, Scotland, U.K.

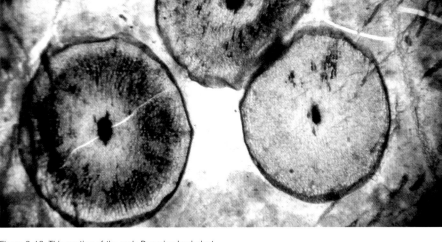

Figure 9-20. Thin section of the early Devonian land plant *Aglaophyton* containing *Palaeomyces gordoni* fungal cysts. *Photo courtesy of K. Davis*

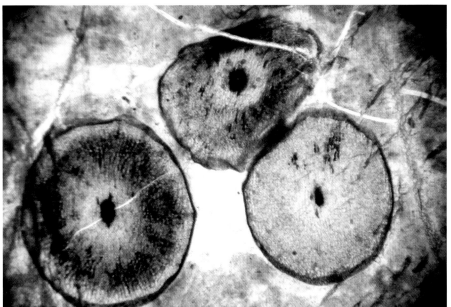

Figure 9-19. Thin section of the early Devonian land plant *Aglaophyton. Photo courtesy of K. Davis*

"Marl Reef"

In 2013, based on the suggestion of Ed Landing, New York State paleontologist, my wife, Linda, and I visited Green Lake, New York. We were on a stromatolite collecting/photography trip to the East Coast and decided to check out Green Lake. Our first impression was, "What a beautiful lake and setting." Glaciers formed Green Lake and its nearby neighbor, Round Lake, some 10,000 years ago. Green Lake has a maximum depth of 195 feet and a gorgeous blue turquoise color. There is a nice path all the way around the lake. Near the pavilion at the east end, a sign informed us of the presence of a "marl reef" in Green Lake. We had never heard of a marl reef, so we

"Reefs" in Central New York?

As you hike the lake trails in the park, observe the white, chalky deposits in shallow water near the shoreline of both lakes. Particularly interesting is the terrace "reef" at Deadman's Point in Green Lake, which is exposed when the lake level is low. Scientists call such reefs "microbialites," meaning that they are constructed by living organisms. The reefs are composed mostly of marl, which is mainly calcium carbonate bound to small cyanobacteria.

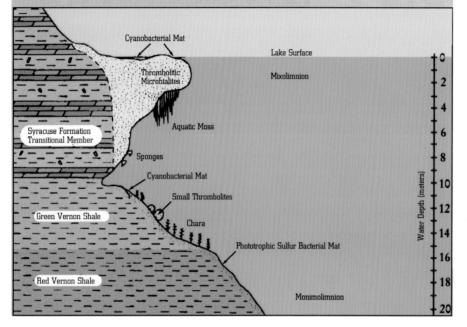

Figure 9-22. Deadman's Point, Green Lakes State Park, with a portion of the "marl reef" just below the water's surface.

Figure 9-21. A sign at Green Lakes State Park, New York, with a diagram depicting what the "marl reef" looks like below the water. *Image and design layout courtesy of the New York State Office of Parks, Recreation and Historic Preservation (NYS-OPRHP) Central Region*

set out to see it. A short distance down the path, we encountered Deadman's Point and the living "reef." Two signs at the park explained how the reef formed and continues to form. The following is quoted from the sign "Deadman's Point: an Ancient but Living 'Reef.'"

Dubbed Deadman's Point, this large "reef" is partially exposed when the lake level is low. It is the best example of a shoreline "reef" formation at Green Lakes State Park. These white, chalky, reef-like, shoreline formations began thousands of years ago when the lakes were being formed. The "reefs" are composed of a substance called marl, which is mainly calcium carbonate (a form of limestone) bound to tiny bacteria. The "reefs" increase in size as the bacteria precipitate more calcium carbonate. This process creates a beautiful underwater scene as algae, mosses, sponges, and fallen trees become encrusted.

Another of the signs, shown in Figure 9-21, shows that the reef is made up of cyanobacteria, thrombolitic microbialites, cyanobacterial mats, and small thrombolites. Near the bottom of the formation is a phototrophic sulfur bacterial mat. All these organisms are certainly stromatolite or stromatolitic and very much fall into the purview of this book.

Upon returning home, I talked on the phone with Mark Teece, a professor at New York State University, Syracuse,

New York. Dr. Teece was kind enough to email me the underwater photos you see here illustrating the microbialites that help to make up the reef. We found Green Lake to be well worth our stop as it is beautiful, educational, and the reef itself seems to draw you to it with an almost alien allure. It is fascinating to know this is a living and growing formation with just enough showing to make one want to learn more.

Figure 9-23. Deadman's Point, Green Lakes State Park, New York, with an exposed surface of the "marl reef."

Figure 9-24. Submerged log covered with microbialites at Deadman's Point, Green Lakes State Park, New York.

Figure 9-25. Underwater look at some of the microbialites which help to form the "marl reef" at Green Lakes State Park. *Photo courtesy of Mark Teece*

Figure 9-26. Another photo of some of the microbialites at Green Lakes State Park, New York. *Photo courtesy of Mark Teece*

Pink Lake on the West Coast of Australia

Returning to Perth, Australia, after our 2013 visit to Shark Bay, we made a detour to check out what our travel brochure described as a pink lake. This pink lake is on the West Coast of Australia near Port Gregory. Traveling on George Grey Road, we encountered what is known as Hutt Lagoon. Hutt Lagoon is a body of very saline water approximately 8.7 miles long, 1.2 miles wide, and 2.2 feet deep. The lagoon is separated from the Indian Ocean by a beach barrier ridge and barrier sand dune. Our first impression of the pink lake was that it appeared rather crusty, but it did indeed have a pink tone. Upon learning that the pink appearance was due to algae and bacteria, I thought this would make for an interesting addition to this chapter.

From what I could determine, the intensity of the lake's pink color depends on the salinity of the water, the temperature (higher temps = more pink), and the light intensity. These factors are more favorable in summer, and we were there in early fall. In the summer the salinity, temperatures, and light intensity all increase and the resident algae/bacteria have to adapt or would die. The two main species of algae/bacteria in the lagoon are *Dunalella sailina* and *Halobacteria cutirubrum*. In the summer, the algae begin to produce beta-carotene, a reddish-orange organic pigment that helps protect them from the adverse effects of extreme summer conditions. The concentration of carotenoids and the pink halobacteria that accumulate in the salt on the lagoon bottom give the water its pink appearance.

This pink lake phenomenon occurs several other places in the world, including Senegal and Canada.

Figure 9-27. Hutt Lagoon is a salt lake with a pink hue on the west coast of Australia near Port Gregory.

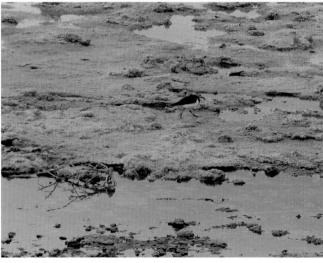

Figure 9-28. Portions of the pink lake, Hutt Lagoon, have crusty surfaces with a ruddy turnstone walking on its surface.

Figure 9-29. Hutt Lagoon exhibiting its characteristic pink appearance. The pink color is brighter in the summer when the temperature and light intensity are greater.

Calcareous Tufa

Recently, while driving through the Black Hills of South Dakota, I stopped at a rock shop to look for stromatolites. While I didn't find any stromatolites, I did find something called tufa. I was told that the intriguing piece of material came from near Hot Springs, South Dakota. Though ugly-looking, it intrigued me enough that I bought several pieces.

When I got home I did some research and concluded that it deserved to be in this book. One source described tufa as highly porous sedimentary rock (limestone) composed of calcium carbonate, $CaCO_3$. Another definition says it is a porous rock composed of calcium carbonate and formed by precipitation from water such as from mineral springs. Tufa's porosity is a result of indigenous plants such as mosses, leaves, green algae, or reeds, which are covered by carbonates. Tufas are usually found in deposits of cool spring waters, but may also be found in warm water springs like those at Hot Springs, South Dakota. These springs are usually supersaturated with calcium bicarbonate. The precipitation of carbonates in these calcium-rich deposits is assisted by the photosynthesis of phototrophic microbes and plants. Tufa's color is derived from minerals, mainly iron oxide, and is usually brown, sometimes yellow or reddish.

Figure 9-30. Chunk of tufa with what appears to be small stromatolites at its base. From Hot Springs, South Dakota, Holocene in age.

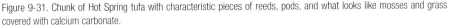

Figure 9-31. Chunk of Hot Spring tufa with characteristic pieces of reeds, pods, and what looks like mosses and grass covered with calcium carbonate.

Figure 9-32. Tufa, calcium carbonate deposits over vegetation, Plio/Pleistocene, collected near Alnif, Atlas Mountains, Morocco.

Figure 9-33. Tufa formed in hot, calcium-rich geothermal water, Pleistocene, Black Rock Desert, Nevada.

Figure 9-34. This specimen of calcium carbonate-coated moss from a spring in eastern Missouri might be called a moss stromatolite and also could be considered another form of tufa. It formed when photosynthesizing moss, growing at the discharge of a spring charged with calcium ions, combined with dissolved carbon dioxide (as carbonic acid). This activity is continuing today at the collection site.

Miscellaneous Specimens with Extremophile Moneran Links

Other intriguing specimens for collection are fossilized remains of hot springs, extremophiles, geothermal vent material, and material from springs and any other rock or mineral of a biogenic or possible biogenic origin.

Extremophiles are organisms that live and thrive in physical or chemically extreme conditions that would deter most other life on Earth. Most, but not all, extremophiles are microbes. The first hot spring bacteria were identified in the 1960s and in 1977, when deep-sea vent communities were discovered. The discovery of extremophile organisms has greatly expanded the range of life habitats on Earth and perhaps beyond. Certainly there are theories and conjecture that extremophile organisms may have been the origin of life on Earth. Since extremophiles can tolerate such harsh and foreign environments, there is the possibility of microbial life on other planets.

The fossilized remains of geothermal, extremophile, or other biogenic material can be quite beautiful when cut and polished. This material is formed and found in association with bacteria and algae. Whether a carbon footprint can be found in these materials or not, we do know that bacteria was involved in their formation. Bacteria precipitated the calcium carbonate, minerals, and other substances found in the fossilized remains. Not all of these formations can be called stromatolites, but many are stromatolitic in nature.

Figure 9-35. Sphalerite from Olkusz, Olkusz District, Milopolskie, Poland. Sphalerite is formed by bacteria that exists in regions with low oxygen solution (O_2) such as flooded tunnels. The bacteria combine zinc and sulfur from the water to create a byproduct of sphalerite. The sulfide usually reacts with elements such as zinc to create insoluble products. The buildup of this microbial precipitation from older generations of bacteria underground might explain the discovery of large zinc sulfide deposits by miners. The biofilm found in such areas appears gray, which coincides with the natural development of sphalerite.

Figure 9-36. A small sphalerite specimen, similar to the Polish specimen, Waukesha Formation, Racine County, Racine, Wisconsin. This sphalerite was probably formed similar to the Polish piece and is probably Silurian in age.

Figure 9-37. Sulfur crystals from Monroe County, Maybee, Michigan, possibly Mesozoic in age. This probably formed as a result of bacterial reduction of preexisting sulfate minerals such as anhydrite and gypsum.

Figure 9-38. Possible extremophile stromatolite, Pleistocene in age, from the Black Rock Desert of Nevada. Probably formed in a geyser-like structure or hot spring deposit.

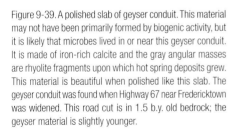

Figure 9-39. A polished slab of geyser conduit. This material may not have been primarily formed by biogenic activity, but it is likely that microbes lived in or near this geyser conduit. It is made of iron-rich calcite and the gray angular masses are rhyolite fragments upon which hot spring deposits grew. This material is beautiful when polished like this slab. The geyser conduit was found when Highway 67 near Fredericktown was widened. This road cut is in 1.5 b.y. old bedrock; the geyser material is slightly younger.

Figure 9-40. Biogenic extremophile activity in association with opal deposit. Calcium carbonate has been replaced by opal, cornelian, and onyx. From the Mexican opal mining district, state of Aquas Calientes, Mexico. Miocene in age.

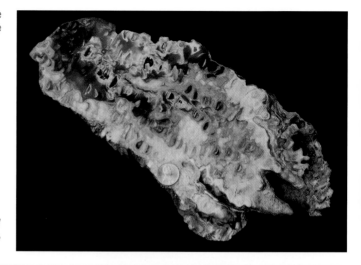

Figure 9-41. Bumble Bee "Jasper"—Travertine, which may have been at least partially formed by thermophiles and extremophiles in geothermal fumaroles (volcanic vents). Pliocene, Garut, Mount Papandyay Volcano, Java, Indonesia.

Figure 9-42. This specimen is "classic" gossan, or iron cap. Gossan is intensely oxidized, weathered, and decomposed rock. All that remains are iron oxides and quartz in the form of "boxworks," quartz-lined cavities retaining the shape of the dissolved ore minerals. Collected in Wood County, Wisconsin, this rock was associated with a Paleoproterozoic subduction zone between two continental plates. Age is approximately 1.8 b.y. old. Recent research concludes that much of the ore was precipitated out of hydrothermal solution by chemosynthetic, thermophilic, and extremophilic bacteria similar to that which occurs in modern "black smokers" and geothermal vents.

Figure 9-43. Specimen of a "white smoker" from a preserved freshwater vent from ancient Lake Gosiute, Green River, Wyoming, Eocene, 50 m.y.a. Some of the bacteria that lived in this vent and in present day "white smokers" were and are the most primitive organisms on earth. Among the primitive organisms living in these vents were sulfate-reducing thermophilic chemosynthetic bacteria. Some lived as small blobs resembling snow within the rising plume. Others grew as mats or biofilms and were grazed by higher life forms. Chemosynthetic bacteria in "smokers" utilize a process called chemosynthesis, by which inorganic material is synthesized into new compounds with the ability to be used as energy by other organisms or itself. The calcite crystals visible in the fossilized "smoker" were the last minerals to come out of suspension as the lake dried up.

Figure 9-44. Rudolph Grotto Gardens, Rudolph, Wisconsin. A five-acre garden and shrine begun in 1927 and finished in 1983. Father Philip Wagner conceived the idea for this grotto and garden, on property owned by St. Philip Church. Rocks used in the construction came from surrounding farmland and consist primarily of gossan rock.

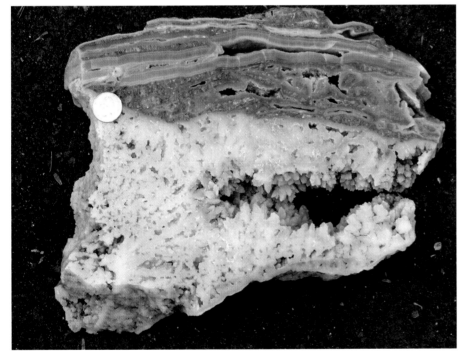

Figure 9-45. A rough gossan rock in the Rudolph Grotto Gardens, Rudolph, Wisconsin.

Figure 9-46. Calcite and travertine from hydrothermal vent, formed by thermophilic bacteria communities. These calcite crystals formed the "roof-cap" of a hydrothermal vent containing the travertine injected into the Lodi Shale. Upper Cambrian near Muscoda, Wisconsin. Discovered and collected in 1994 by Gerald Gunderson.

Glossary

Anhydrate. A compound that is formed from another by the removal of water.

Biofilm. A thin, usually resistant layer of microorganisms (as bacteria) that form on and coat surfaces.

Biogenic. Produced or brought about by living organisms.

Calcite. A common mineral with highly variable forms and colors.

Carbonates. Rocks and other Earth materials that have an abundance of calcium carbonate ($CaCO_3$).

Carotenoids. Any of a class of mainly yellow, orange, or red fat-soluble pigments including carotene.

Chalcedony. A microcrystalline type of quartz occurring in several different forms, including onyx, agate, and jasper; a translucent type of quartz.

Chara. Green algae common in freshwater lakes of limestone districts.

Chert. A hard, dark, opaque rock composed of silica with an amorphous or microscopically fine-grained texture.

Concretions. Hard bodies that form in sediments before they become sedimentary rocks; slow chemical changes, perhaps related to microbial activity, cause minerals to come out of the groundwater and cement sediment together

Dolostone. A sedimentary rock composed mainly of the mineral dolomite, which is magnesium calcium carbonate.

Extremophile. A microorganism, especially archea, that lives in conditions of extreme temperature, acidity, alkalinity, or chemical concentrations.

Ferrous iron. One of the iron oxides, consists of the chemical element iron in an oxidation state of 2 bonded to oxygen, with the chemical formula FeO; also known as iron (II) oxide.

Geothermal. Derived from the heat in Earth's interior.

Gypsum. A common mineral, hydrated calcium sulfate, occurring in crystals and in masses soft enough to be scratched by a fingernail.

Halobacteria. Rod-shaped archaebacteria, as of the genus *Halobacterium* and *Holococcus*, occurring in saline environments.

Meromictic. A lake with layers of water that do not mix. Most lakes physically mix the surface and deep water at least once per year. The lack of mixing creates very different environments for organism to live in.

Microbes. Microorganisms or bacteria.

Microbial mat. A multilayered sheet of microorganisms, mainly bacteria and archaea.

Microbialite. Organosedimentary structures formed by microorganisms that are usually photosynthetic, through binding and trapping of sediment and/or precipitation of minerals.

Mixolimnion. The upper layer of a meromictic lake characterized by low density and free circulation; this layer is mixed by the wind.

Monimolimnion. Dense bottom stratum of a meromictic lake; it is stagnant and does not mix with the water above.

Silica. A hard, unreactive, colorless compound that occurs as the mineral quartz and as a principal constituent of sandstone and other rocks.

Photosynthesis. A metabolic process carried out by photosynthetic bacteria, cyanobacteria, and plants in which light energy is converted to chemical energy and stored in molecules of carbohydrates.

Phototrophic. An organism obtaining energy from sunlight to synthesize organic compounds for nutrition.

Silicified. The process in which organic matter becomes saturated with silica.

Travertine. A calcium carbonate mineral deposit.

Thrombolites. Clotted accretionary structures found in shallow water. Caused by the trapping, binding, and cementation of sedimentary grains by biofilms of microorganisms, especially cyanobacteria.

Bibliography

Esperance–Natural Attractions. 2007. Flyer picked up in Australia with similar information online at www.visitesperance.com/pages/natural-attractions.

Evans, James E. 1999. "Recognition and implications of Eocene tufas and travertines in the Chadron Formation, White River Group, Badlands of South Dakota." *Sedimentology*, 46:771-789.

Handford, C. Robertson. 1991. "Marginal Marine Halite: Sabkhas and Salinas." in *Evaporites, Petroleum and Mineral Resources, Developments in Sedimentology, Vol. 50*, edited by Judith L. Melvin.

Selden, Paul A., and John R. Nudds. 2005. *Evolution of Fossil Ecosystems*. Chicago: University of Chicago Press, pp 47-58.

Chapter Ten

Where and How to Find Stromatolites

R. J. Leis

So you are interested in stromatolites and are asking, "Where might I find them?" Well-fossilized stromatolites are distributed world-wide, including Antarctica. It is always fun and adventurous to try to find them in their natural surroundings. However, not all of us are able or willing to go afield.

A local rock shop got me started collecting fossils (see Preface). Rock shops are not as common as they once were, but some are still around. So whenever you are near a rock shop, stop in and ask the proprietor if they have any stromatolites; a better approach might be to ask for "fossilized algae." However, I have found stromatolites in rock shops even after the person behind the counter claimed they don't have any. Poke around and look in drawers, and you just might find a stromatolite or two. You might ask for a deal on a stromatolite you find on your own, since the proprietor probably doesn't think it's important if he didn't even know it was there.

Another way to observe fossilized stromatolites or add to your collection is to attend local, national, or international gem, mineral, and fossil shows. Every state has one or more of these shows annually. The shows are heavy on the gem and mineral aspects of geo-collectibles, but there are usually one or two fossil dealers. Here again, ask if they have stromatolites, or just browse on your own. I have picked up many fine stromatolite specimens at gem,

Figure 10-1. Enchanted Garden Rock Shop, Richfield, Minnesota, where I discovered and purchased my first stromatolite.

Figure 10-2. Dan Damrow, Rib River Fossils, Mosinee, Wisconsin, and one of the many fossil shows he attends. Dan is perhaps the greatest purveyor of stromatolites nationwide, and I have obtained many fine specimens from him.

Figure 10-3. Stromatolites displayed at Dan Damrow's booth at the ESCONI (Earth Science Club of Northern Illinois) show in Wheaton, Illinois.

Figure 10-4. R. Leis, checking out a display of Moroccan stromatolites at the Tucson, Arizona, Gem, Mineral, and Fossil Show.

Figure 10-5. Crystal World features a large display of Australian stromatolites and BIF at the Tucson, Arizona, annual Gem, Mineral, and Fossil Show.

nice stromatolite displays and to larger museums with no stromatolites. This disparity seems to correlate with the amount of interest the museum curators have in stromatolites. Museums can give you clues to where to find your own stromatolites. Many museums display stromatolites from the nearby area and identify each specimen's general location. This information can be a starting point for collecting on your own. Consider taking photos for reference if you do decide to collect.

Rarely are stromatolites for sale in museum gift shops, but it is worth a look. I have also found that you might be able to work out a trade if you can find the right person. However, it may take persistence to find a museum employee with the interest and authority to make a trade.

Stromatolites can sometimes be found in construction material and in the places that sell it, although store owners will likely not be aware of the biogenic origin of their rocks. Stromatolites may be found on building blocks, signs, benches, countertops, and landscaping rocks. In years past, buildings were constructed out of available local materials in fields and quarries, and sometimes they were stromatolitic.

The Internet is another good source of stromatolites. Fossilmall.com has five online fossil stores, and most sell stromatolites. The site also posts good information on stromatolites. You can also buy them on e-Bay, though I haven't been as satisfied with them; often the age or collection site is not given.

The most interesting way to obtain stromatolites is to collect them yourself. I liken stromatolite collecting to hunting. You have to locate your prey, identify it, bag it, retrieve it, prepare it, and then display it. I have collected several "trophy" or museum-grade stromatolites on my hunting trips. The biggest difference between hunting and

mineral, and fossil shows. I have also found that dealers at these shows are willing to strike a bargain with you. You might also ask where the fossils came from. Sometimes, especially if you buy something, a dealer will share information on where to collect.

Dates for the three largest gem, mineral, and fossil shows, which are in Tucson, Arizona; Denver, Colorado; and Springfield, Massachusetts; can be found on Martin Zinn Expositions website, www.mzexpos.com.

Natural history museums are good places to observe fossilized stromatolites. I have been to small museums with

Figure 10-6. R. Leis's personal museum containing more than 700 specimens of stromatolites, BIF, and other material of a biogenic origin.

Figure 10-8. Another view from the Sam Noble Natural History Museum, Hall of Ancient Life exhibit.

Figure 10-7. Sam Noble Natural History Museum, University of Oklahoma, Oklahoma City, Oklahoma. At the start of the Hall of Ancient Life exhibit are dioramas, stromatolites, and excellent information on stromatolites and other primitive life forms. This exhibit takes you on a tour of four billion years of Oklahoma prehistory. Chase Studios of Cedar Creek, Missouri, designed this exhibit, which I found most engaging.

Figure 10-9. One of the stromatolites exhibited at the Salt Lake City, Utah, Natural History Museum. It is a stromatolite cross section covered with caddisfly cases collected near Sweet Water County, Wyoming.

Figure 10-10. Mural depicting what an Archean stromatolite scene may have looked like. This mural can be seen at the Smithsonian Museum of Natural History, Washington, DC. *Photo courtesy of Tom R. Johnson*

Figure 10-11. A mounted slab of one of the oldest fossil stromatolites known to date. This 3.4 b.y. old stromatolite is from the Pilbara Region, Western Australia at the Smithsonian, Washington, DC. *Photo courtesy of Tom R. Johnson*

Figure 10-12. My friend, Tom R. Johnson, at the Smithsonian, Washington, DC, giving some perspective to a huge slab of 1.8 b.y. old banded iron from Jasper Knob, Ishpeming, Michigan. *Photo courtesy of Tom R. Johnson*

Figure 10-13. Mike Riesch of the Earth Haven Museum, Gillett, Wisconsin. He is standing next to a display of stromatolites, mainly from Wisconsin and the Midwest. This small museum has a larger display of stromatolites than are found in some larger museums of natural history.

stromatolite collecting is that you are not killing anything, and no license fee is required.

I realize that some people consider geologic collecting improper or even unethical. However, I believe that if you respect private land and comply with federal, state, and local laws, there should be no problem. In most instances the stromatolite formations are vast or in an erosional state, and collecting them will not deplete the supply. Also, weathering, either natural or man-made, may very well exceed any limited collecting, and some of the best "stroms" are found loose on the stromatolite outcrop. Fossilized stromatolites are abundant, and collecting them only increases their appreciation and educational value.

Figure 10-14. Mike Riesch outside the Earth Haven Museum alongside a huge collection of Ordovician stromatolites from nearby quarries.

Figure 10-15. Shell, Wyoming, post office. I knew I might be on the right track when we found their display mailbox surrounded by stromatolites.

Figure 10-16. R. Leis packing stromatolites in US Postal Service flat-rate boxes. This is an economical way of getting your stromatolites home.

Once I locate an area that looks promising, I like to go to the nearest town and ask where to find the stromatolites. Usually someone knows about nearby fossils and is happy to share where to find them. I have had good luck going to the local post office and asking the postmaster for the names of knowledgeable locals. Small-town postmasters seem to know everyone in town and can often direct you to the local "rock person." Sometimes this "rock person" will be so impressed by your interest that he will offer to show you where to find specimens. If the location is on private land, schmoozing often results in permission to look; if not, look for a nearby public location.

I carry a certain amount of equipment into the field. A 4×4 vehicle can be useful, but I have been on many successful collecting trips with just my Prius. Here are the items I take with me: drinking water, chigger and mosquito spray, crow bar (bright color), rock hammer, mallet, leather gloves, eye protection, rain gear, box for rocks, tarp, GPS, camera, sunscreen, rubberbands, 3×5 card (to rubber band to specimen), notepad, markers, backpack, strapping tape, *World's Oldest Fossils* book, and now this book. If you are successful in collecting stromatolites and don't want to haul them around in your car, go back to the post office; ask the postal workers for a large, flat-rate shipping box, and send them home.

Figure 10-17. A closer look at the stromatolites around the Shell, Wyoming, mailbox. The postmaster directed us to the local rock expert, who gave us tips on where to collect.

Once you get your specimens home, it is fun to display them. The true beauty of stromatolites often can only be seen when they are cut and polished; however, the tools to do that are expensive. If you do not want to invest in equipment, consider paying someone who has a rock saw and polisher to prepare your specimen. Collectors and rock shop owners are potential sources for cutting and polishing. You may work out a mutually agreed upon stromatolite swap if they are interested in your specimens. A common

exchange is 50 percent for the collector and 50 percent for the person with the saw. If they are polishing the cut slabs, you will receive less in return, as the polishing operation is time-consuming. You always hope to garner more than one finished piece of stromatolite so that you will have trading material and thus be able to expand your collection.

However and wherever you do your collecting, please do it in a legal, moderate, courteous, clean, and safe manner so as to leave a good impression for future collectors.

Figure 10-18. An approximately two-foot-by-three-foot, strikingly beautiful stromatolite. This specimen is from the Phosphoria Formation, Big Horn County, Shell, Wyoming, and is 240 m.y. old.

Figure 10-19. Linda Leis holding a specimen of Phosphoria stromatolite from Shell, Wyoming. In the background are the rolling grasslands where this material is found.

Figure 10-20. View from the summit of Douglas Pass, Garfield County, Colorado, elevation 8,265 feet above sea level. Many Green River Formation stromatolites can be found near the summit of this pass.

Figure 10-21. An example of an Eocene Green River Formation stromatolite that can be found on Douglas Pass.

Figure 10-22. Owl Butte, Butte County, south of Highway 212, northeast of Newell, South Dakota. This is an area where one can find Eocene stromatolites approximately 37 m.y. old. Geologists believe they formed in a large freshwater or brackish lake.

Figure 10-23. Specimen of an Eocene age stromatolite from the Newell area found in riprap near a culvert under Highway 212.

Figure 10-24. R. Leis sitting on a 1 b.y. old Precambrian freshwater stromatolite. This photo was taken at Horseshoe Harbor, Mary MacDonald Nature Conservancy Preserve, Keweenaw County, Michigan. Lake Superior is in the background, and the site is breathtakingly beautiful.

Figure 10-25. Close-up of one of the stromatolite formations at Horseshoe Harbor, Michigan.

Figure 10-26. Terry McKee and R. Leis on the edge of Delaney Rim, Sweetwater County, near Wamsutter, Wyoming. We are examining specimens of the Green River Formation. Masses of Eocene-age stromatolite fragments are found along the entire length of the ridge.

Figure 10-27. This photo shows how pervasive and extensive the stromatolites are on Delaney Rim.

Figure 10-28. A field littered with stromatolites from the Cool Creek Formation, Arbuckle Mountains near Ardmore, Oklahoma. Ordovician in age, most of what you see here are stromatolites primarily consisting of limestone. They protrude from the bedrock and are quite immovable.

Figure 10-29. A closer look at one of the Cool Creek stromatolite "heads" protruding from the ground. These stromatolites are readily accessible at Turner Falls, a public park owned and operated by the city of Davis, Oklahoma. Studies have revealed several morphologies in these stromatolites including thrombolites, digitate forms, columns and domes.

Figure 10-30. R. Leis examining a block of material used in the construction of a concession stand at Turner Falls Park, Oklahoma. Most, if not all, of the stone components of this building are made of fossilized stromatolite rock.

Figure 10-31. Approximate twenty-foot-high outcrop of a stromatolite dome in the middle of a housing complex in Hamburg, New Jersey, Sussex County. It is next to a sidewalk and very accessible.

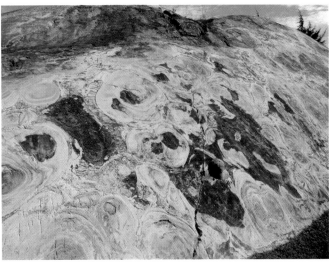

Figure 10-32. Close-up of the stromatolite "heads" on the Hamburg formation. The host rock for this site consists of Allentown Dolomite and is Lower Ordovician-Upper Cambrian in age. This surface of the formation is smooth and has been glacially polished.

Figure 10-33. Back side of the Hamburg stromatolite outcrop.

Figure 10-34. R. Leis examines an outcrop from the Forelle Limestone Member, Lykins Formation. The Lykins Formation covers a large portion of the front range of the Rockies from New Mexico to Wyoming. This particular outcrop is in the Garden of the Gods, Colorado Springs, Colorado, and is Upper Permian in age.

Figure 10-35. Another Lykins Formation specimen. The Forelle Limestone Member contains wavy-pattern stromatolites consisting of algal mats and stromatolites. They were laid down in what may have been an intertidal continental shelf lagoon with shallow pools of hyper-saline water.

Figure 10-36. A stromatolite from St. Lawrence County, near Balmat, New York. This is a stromatolite from the Adirondack Mountains, an area where, until recently, stromatolites were presumed not to exist. This specimen is upside down, indicating folding of the rock during the Grenville Orogeny, and is approximately 1.3 b.y. old.

Figure 10-37. Another photo of the Adirondack stromatolites from a road cut just north of Balmat, New York. These Mesoproterozoic stromatolites are tilted and highly metamorphosed.

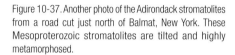

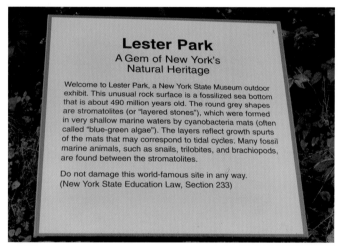

Figure 10-38. Sign at the Lester Park geologic exhibit near Saratoga Springs, New York. A natural history site of the New York State Museum, this park is devoted to stromatolites. This is the type locality for *Cryptozoan*.

Figure 10-39. *Cryptozoan proliferium*. Weathered, glaciated surface of a 490–500 m.y. old fossilized sea floor in Lester Park, with many large and small Hoyt-Limestone stromatolites.

Figure 10-40. Another photo of the Lester Park stromatolites. These New York stromatolites were the first to be described in North America and are perhaps the most photographed in the United States.

Figure 10-41. R. Leis, and Terry McKee next to an approximately 2.4 b.y. old stromatolite near Libby Lake, Nash Fork Formation, Snowy Range, Medicine Bow Mountains, Wyoming.

Figure 10-42. Linda Leis standing next to a vertical bed of stromatolitic (or algal) limestone of the Nash Formation of the Medicine Bow Mountains, Wyoming. Domes and reefs composed of marine stromatolites litter the Medicine Bow Mountains near Libby Lake. Even after continent-forming metamorphism and mountain-building events, the stromatolite structure is still clearly evident in these rocks.

Figure 10-43. Large stromatolites in early Proterozoic (Paleoproterozoic) Nash Limestone of the Medicine Bow Mountains of Wyoming. These large "stroms" were first brought to the attention of fossil aficionados in *The Fossil Book,* by C. L. and M. A. Fenton.

Figure 10-44. Large stromatolites in the 2.4 b.y. old Nash Limestone covered with orange lichens, an appropriate combination as lichens represent a symbiosis between cyanobacteria and fungi.

Figure 10-45. Beds of iron formation in early Proterozoic rocks of the Medicine Bow Mountains, Wyoming.

Figure 10-46. A closer look at one of the deeply weathered and metamorphosed stromatolites from the Snowy Range, Medicine Bow Mountains, Wyoming.

Figure 10-47. Upper Cambrian, limestone stromatolite, Frederick County, near Frederick, Maryland.

Figure 10-48. The Walkersville Heritage Farm Park, Frederick County, Maryland, have utilized many of these Upper Cambrian stromatolites to restrict parking and direct the flow of traffic in the park.

Figure 10-49. Thrombolite, reef-like outcrop in Frederick County, Hagerstown, Maryland, Stonehenge Formation, early Ordovician in age.

Figure 10-50. Along Highway 65 between Hagerstown and Antietam National Battle Field are outcrops of the Conococheague Formation, thrombolite/stromatolites, Upper Cambrian in age. The US Park Service has utilized stromatolitic rocks from the Conococheague Formation in the building of stone fences at the Antietam Battlefield.

Figure 10-51. A couple of the thrombolite/stromatolitic rocks that have been use in the Antietam Battlefield fence works.

Figure 10-52. The Casque Isles Trail at Schreiber, Ontario, is where you can begin your hike to see the famous Lake Superior stromatolite rings. From Schreiber beach it is an approximately six-mile round trip, a rugged hike to the stromatolites, but well worth the effort.

Figure 10-53. Concentric stromatolite rings in rocks of the 1.8–1.9 b.y. old Gunflint Formation. The rings vary in size, with the largest being a little more than three feet in diameter; they cover an area of several hundred square yards.

Figure 10-54. Close-up look at one of the stromatolite rings, which are made up of iron-rich cherty rocks.

Figure 10-55. Another view of the Schreiber Channel stromatolites. While it was exciting to view the stromatolite formations, the natural beauty of the rocks and Lake Superior were equally rewarding.

Figure 10-56. R. Leis on the stromatolite rings, which contain fossil bacteria and a variety of other diverse microfossils.

Figure 10-57. Geologists B. Stinchcomb and Jose Garcia examining 1.5 b.y. old *Ozarkcollenia* specimens on Cuthbertson Mountain, Iron County, Missouri.

Figure 10-58. *Ozarkcollenia* specimens being collected on Cuthbertson Mountain, Missouri.

Figure 10-59. Overseer Tom Nash and R. Leis viewing the abandoned Steep Rock Iron Mine, which is filling with water, at Atikoken, Ontario, Canada.

Figure 10-60. Archean stromatolite domes at the Atikoken Steep Rock Iron Mine.

Figure 10-61. Close-up of one of the stromatolite domes of the Steep Rock Iron Mine. This stromatolite's signature is clearly evident despite its being nearly 3 b.y. old.

Figure 10-62. R. Leis, and T. McKee with a museum-grade large piece of Pennsylvanian age stromatolite, Eagle County, Colorado.

Figure 10-63. The top of this mountain is where the Eagle County stromatolite came from. No easy task getting this stromatolite off the mountain, but worth the effort.

Figure 10-64. R. Leis and T. McKee in an Archean stromatolite-strewn gully, Goshen County near Hartville, Wyoming.

Figure 10-65. Archean stromatolite, 2.58 b.y. old, of the Upper Whalen Group, Hartville Uplift, near Hartville, Wyoming. These stromatolites are highly metamorphosed and occur in dolomitic marbles.

Figure 10-66. Large stromatolite near Redcliff Island, north end of Great Slave Lake, Northwest Territories, Canada. This stromatolitic rock is approximately 15–20 feet long. *Photo courtesy of Tom R. Johnson*

Figure 10-67. Close-up of a tilted stromatolite illustrating its distinctive stromatolite laminations. Great Slave Lake, Northwest Territories, Canada. *Photo courtesy of Tom R. Johnson*

Figure 10-68. R. Leis and B. Stinchcomb examining a road cut on Highway 63, Texas County near Licking, Missouri. The road cuts through the Roubidoux Formation and is Lower Ordovician in age.

Figure 10-69. A nice, cherty stromatolite, Roubidoux Formation, Lower Ordovician, in road cut on Highway 63, Texas County, near Licking, Missouri.

Figure 10-69a. The author providing scale to an outstanding stromatolite formation in Glacier National Park, Montana. This Precambrian formation is adjacent to the Going to the Sun Highway. It is approximately 1.5 b.y. old and is from the Siyeh Limestone Formation of the Belt Supergroup.

Figure 10-70. You never know where you might find stromatolites. These Ordovician, Oneota Formation stromatolites were being used as decorative rock in a flower garden near Norwalk, Wisconsin.

Figure 10-71. Another look at the incorporation of stromatolites in a flower garden near Norwalk, Wisconsin. Where stromatolites are abundant, you may find them being sold at garden centers as decorative rock.

Figure 10-72. A druzy-covered stromatolite accenting a beautiful flower garden in Mosinee, Wisconsin. This stromatolite is from the abandoned barite mine, Washington County, Missouri, and is Cambrian in age. This quartz material formed in cavities of these ancient stromatolites and can be beautiful, as shown here in a garden setting. *Photo courtesy of Cynthia Damrow*

Figure 10-73. Philip Burgess, surrounded by Oneota Formation stromatolites decorating his yard in Prairie du Chien, Wisconsin. Phil describes himself as a knowledgeable amateur paleontologist, and he is an authority on the Oneota Formation of Southwestern Wisconsin and Southeastern Minnesota.

Figure 10-74. A planar or *Stratifera* St. Croix Valley Limestone stromatolite vein cut, recently quarried by Rivard Stone, Somerset, Wisconsin, Oneota Formation, Lower Ordovician in age.

Figure 10-76. Rivard Stone sells many tons of the stromatolite for use as blocks in building construction. The Cottage Grove, Minnesota, Government Center is partially constructed of this distinctive stromatolite. The background blocks, shown here in the Council Chamber, are also made of St. Croix Valley Somerset stromatolite.

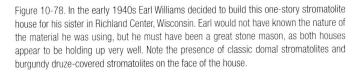

Figure 10-78. In the early 1940s Earl Williams decided to build this one-story stromatolite house for his sister in Richland Center, Wisconsin. Earl would not have known the nature of the material he was using, but he must have been a great stone mason, as both houses appear to be holding up very well. Note the presence of classic domal stromatolites and burgundy druze-covered stromatolites on the face of the house.

Figure 10-75. Rivard Stone sign utilizing the St. Croix Valley Limestone Somerset Oneota Formation stromatolite. Many of the surrounding businesses have signs such as this made from stromatolite.

Figure 10-77. In the late 1930s Earl Williams constructed this distinctive stromatolite fieldstone house in rural Viola, Wisconsin. Earl used Oneota Formation, Prairie du Chien Group, Ordovician stromatolites from the surrounding neighbors' properties. One of Earl's descendents still lives in this one-of-a-kind house.

Figure 10-79. Close-up of some of the *Cryptozoan* and druze quartz-covered stromatolites used in the construction of the Richland Center stromatolite house.

Figure 10-80. Stromatolite-lined embankment at the garage entrance of the Richland Center stromatolite house.

Figure 10-81. Covering the Cabool High School at Cabool, Missouri, are stones containing stromatolites, ripple marks, and desiccation cracks. This material was gathered from the surrounding area and is lower Ordovician in age. This building and many others in Cabool and surrounding cities is an example of the 1930s Ozark Giraffe Style architecture. This type of architecture consists of stone slabs with extremely wide mortar between the stones, creating a pattern that reminds one of a giraffe.

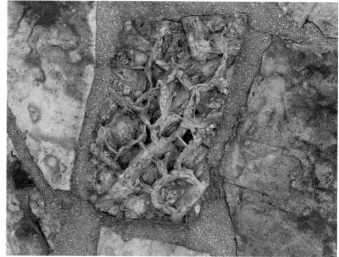

Figure 10-82. Close-up of deep desiccation cracks on the Cabool High School. The desiccation cracks probably formed by shrinkage of moneran mats when exposed to the air at low tide.

Glossary

Dolomite. Sedimentary carbonate rock and a mineral compound of calcium carbonate, usually gray in color.

Intertidal. Where land and sea meet, covered by water at high tide and uncovered at low tide

Metadolomitic. A metamorphic dolomite or dolomite marble.

Metamorphosed. Recrystallization of an existing rock typically occurs at high temperatures and high pressure.

Orogeny. The process of mountain-making or upheaval.

Bibliography

Clos, Lynne M. 2008. *North America Through Time: A Paleontological History of Our Continent*. Publisher: Fossil News.

Elmore, R. Douglas. 1983. "Precambrian non-marine stromatolites in alluvial fan deposits, the Copper Harbor Conglomerate, upper Michigan." *Sedimentology*, 30:829-842.

Hofmann, Hans J., and George L. Snyder. 1985. "Archean stromatolites from the Hartville Uplift, eastern Wyoming." *Geological Society of America Bulletin*, 96:842-849.

Knight, Samuel H., and David Keefer. 2004. "Preliminary report on the Precambrian stromatolites in the Nash Formation, Medicine Bow Mountains Wyoming." *Rocky Mountain Geology*, 5:1-11.

Chapter Eleven

Present-Day Stromatolites

R.J. Leis

After exploring fossilized stromatolites in chapter 5, it is now time to view some of the present-day living stromatolites. Prior to 1956 and the discovery of stromatolites at Shark Bay in Western Australia, it was thought that distinctive stromatolites were extinct. It is truly amazing, when you think about it, that such organic structures as stromatolites could have existed from the beginning of life some 3.5 billion years ago to the present. What's even more astounding is how these stromatolites could have survived the many climate and environmental changes of the last several billion years and still remain relatively the same to this day.

After stromatolites were discovered at Shark Bay, they have since been found in many other locations around the world, in both freshwater and saltwater. These places include Yellowstone National Park in Wyoming, the Bahamas, Brazil, Antarctic lakes, Spain, the Yucatan Peninsula of Mexico, Chetunal Bay in Belize, Lake Salda in Turkey, Pavillion Lake, and Lake Killy in British Columbia. I have been told there are several lakes in Wisconsin and Minnesota that contain freshwater stromatolites, but their location is not being revealed to the public to protect the stromatolites and their habitat.

Bahamian "Stroms"

Stromatolites are rare in today's oceans, unlike during the Precambrian Era. Currently, ocean-dwelling living stromatolites are found in two places—the Bahamas and Hamelin Pool at Shark Bay, Australia.

The Bahamian stromatolites, first discovered in the 1980s, are unique in that they are the only known present-day stromatolites growing in the open ocean. They are

Figure 11-1. Stromatolites at Bock Cay, Bahamas. *Photo courtesy of R. Pamela Reid, University of Miami*

found in several locations along Exuma Sound. The Bahamian stromatolites were thought to have begun forming from one to two thousand years ago. These stromatolites are an exception to the belief that stromatolites can only form in locations devoid of predators or grazers. The Bahamian stromatolites exist in open oceans because of the tremendous tidal currents and sand waves that occur off the Bahamas. These currents and sand waves preclude other life from forming where the stromatolites develop. The Bahamian stromatolites are composed primarily of fine-grained ooid sand (the granules are made of calcium carbonate and are smaller than 2 mm, 0.08 inch, in diameter) that is trapped

Figure 11-2. Stromatolites at Bock Cay, Bahamas. Bahamian stromatolites primarily consist of fine grained (≤2 mm, 0.08 inches) carbonate sand, called ooid sand, that is trapped and cemented by the cyanobacteria, *Schizothrix* sp. The fine ooid sand has visibly drifted at the base of these stromatolites. *Photo courtesy of R. Pamela Reid, University of Miami*

Figure 11-3. Stromatolites at Little Darby Cay, Bahamas. The columnar morphology of this stromatolite is visible in this photo. *Photo courtesy of R. Pamela Reid, University of Miami*

Figure 11-4. Stromatolites at Little Darby Cay, Bahamas. Note the ooid sand, which can drift up to three feet deep due to strong currents in the sound. Ooid sand is round and composed of calcium carbonate coating a tiny nuclear fragment of shell or bone. The organic calcium carbonate coats the nucleus over time as it is washed about by the currents in a process similar to that of oncolite formation. *Photo courtesy of R. Pamela Reid, University of Miami*

and bound by filamentous cyanobacteria, *Schizothrix* sp. The most common morphology of Bahamian stromatolites is columnar with heights varying from approximately one inch to eight feet. The growth rate of these stromatolites is believed to be less than one millimeter a year, just as those of Shark Bay in Australia. How these open ocean Bahamian stromatolites form is explained in a work titled *Modern Marine Stromatolites of Little Darby Island, Exuma Archipelago, Bahamas.* This detailed and informative publication, complete with many color photographs, was written by R. Pamela Reid, et al., 2011, and is available online. Dr. Reid, of the University of Miami, provided several beautiful photographs for this publication.

Modern "Stroms" in Volcanic Environments

In April of 2013, on a trip of a lifetime, my wife, Linda, and I spent a month touring New Zealand and Australia. While in New Zealand we spent an entire day in one of the most interesting places we have ever visited—Waimangu Volcanic Valley, Rotorua. This volcanic valley seemed to belong in the prehistoric past, yet it is only 129 years old. It formed when mount Tarawera erupted in 1886. Waimangu and its associated Lake Rotomahana is a place of geothermal vents, boiling lakes, hot streams, geysers, strange plants, beautiful algae, and yes, stromatolites. I will attempt to show the flavor of Waimangu with a few photos illustrating its diversity. No photos can duplicate actually being there, since you must also feel the heat and humidity, smell the air, and hear the sounds of the hot springs and streams to truly appreciate the place. This volcanic valley is a definite must-see if you go to New Zealand.

At Waimangu Valley, we photographed what we believe to be stromatolites. They were similar in appearance to the well-documented stromatolites we observed growing

Figure 11-5. Stromatolites forming near a hot spring in the Lower Geyser basin of Yellowstone National Park, Wyoming.

Figure 11-6. Another photo of present-day stromatolites forming near a hot spring in Yellowstone National Park.

Figure 11-7. Stromatolites forming along the cooler edge of Black Pool in the West Thumb Geyser basin of Yellowstone National Park.

Figure 11-8. *Conophyton* (conical) stromatolites formed by the filamentous cyanobacteria *Phormidium sp.*, which are found in hot springs of Yellowstone National Park, Wyoming.

Figure 11-9. What appear to be conical stromatolites having formed at the outlet of Frying Pan Lake, Waimangu Valley, New Zealand. These stromatolites appear similar to those occurring in Yellowstone National Park, Wyoming.

Figure 11-10. Small structures I believe to be stromatolites forming at the cooler edge of Iodine Pool, Waimangu Valley, New Zealand.

Figure 11-11. More stromatolitic-like structures near the relatively cooler edge of Iodine Pool, Waimangu Valley. In this photo it appears that the stromatolitic algae/bacteria may have used a small stick as a nucleus for formation.

near hot springs at Yellowstone National Park in Wyoming. We were privileged to have been able to spend a day at Waimangu, but several days would have been better. Some of the vegetation growing in Waimangu is very interesting and has adapted to the valley's hot and acidic conditions. The heat-loving plants established themselves by natural succession after the 1886 Mount Tarawera eruption.

Figure 11-12. Overview of Iodine Pool, Waimangu Valley, photographing what I believe to be stromatolitic structures forming along the edge of the pool.

Figure 11-13. The relatively cooler edge of Iodine Pool.

Figure 11-14. Stromatolitic-looking structures and the edge of Iodine Pool, Waimangu Valley.

Figure 11-15. A closer look at what I believe to be stromatolites forming on the edge of Iodine Pool, Waimangu Valley.

Figure 11-16. Frying Pan Lake, the world's largest hot spring. The lake covers 38,000 square meters, 9.4 acres, with an average depth of 19.7 feet. The lake temperature is about 131°F.

Figure 11-17. Inferno Crater Lake is a small, pale blue steamy gem of a lake in Waimangu with a fluctuating water level. The lake's depth is 98.4 feet (30 meters) and it's temperature can reach 176°F. The water is highly acidic with a pH as low as 2.1. Inferno Crater is the largest geyser-like feature in the world although the geyser cannot be seen because it is at the bottom of the lake.

Figure 11-18. Fumarole near Frying Pan Lake. The escaping carbon dioxide and hydrogen sulfide gas give the appearance of boiling.

Figure 11-20. Warbrick Terrace is a set of multi-colored, fast-growing silica platforms forming over an old stream terrace in a similar way to Marble Terrace. In recent years, algae have assisted in the silica deposition to build a dam across the stream draining through Rainbow crater.

Figure 11-19. Marble Terrace and Buttresses. These terraces and buttresses are formed by silica depositing out of solution and building in successive layers over time. The beautiful colors seen in this photo are made up of threads and a cushion of blue-green algae intermingled with orange trails of gliding bacterial threads called *chloroflexus*.

Figure 11-21. The prostrate form of Kanuka, (*kunzea ericoides var. microflor*), the light green plant with leaves and thermal arching moss (*Lycophadiella cernus*). Normal Kanuka grows to tree form, but on the hydrothermally heated soils of Waimangu it forms a low shrub with flattened branches. Its roots spread through the top, somewhat cooler, centimeters of soil. When our guide probed a thermometer into this mound of soil where the moss is growing, it read 203°F less than three inches under the moss.

Present-day "Stroms" in Australia

While in Australia we spent a week traveling to and photographing the living stromatolites of Western Australia. Nowhere else in the world are examples of present day stromatolites so dramatic or abundant. We first headed to Lake Clifton, approximately sixty-two miles south of Perth. Lake Clifton is about thirteen miles long and is only a little more than a half-mile wide and very shallow. The deepest part of the lake is not more than three feet. At the north end of the lake, thrombolitic stromatolites form a reef about ninety-eight feet wide and three miles long. These stromatolites vary from fifteen inches to more than a yard across. According to Ken McNamara in his book *Stromatolites*, the water of Lake Clifton is highly saturated in calcium bicarbonate. The microbial communities convert this calcium bicaronate to calcium carbonate in the form of the mineral aragonite. This plentiful supply of calcium carbonate, plus a nutrient-

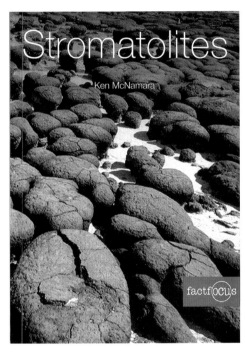

Figure 11-22. *Stromatolites*, by Ken McNamara, is a small book packed with invaluable information about living stromatolites in Australia. Not only does it describe the stromatolites at various locations, it tells you how to find them.

Figure 11-23. Overview of the large formation of thrombolites at Lake Clifton, Western Australia, showing domal-shaped thrombolites that form in moderate depths of Lake Clifton.

Figure 11-24. Flat thrombolites formed in the shallowest parts of Lake Clifton as viewed from the boardwalk.

poor environment, are the two key elements for the occurrence of stromatolites both here and elsewhere south of Perth. The water in which the Lake Clifton stromatolites grow is brackish (that is, the salinity of the water is less than that of the sea). This salinity varies seasonally; it is higher during the summer months as the lake partially evaporates. The Lake Clifton stromatolites are largely the product of the precipitation of calcium carbonate by the filamentous *Cyanobacteria seytonema* sp.

We next traveled to Lake Richmond just south of Rockingham, Australia. Despite being told by the local environmental station to be careful of the venomous tiger snake, we set out to look at the thrombolitic stromatolites. Lake Richmond stromatolites look similar to the Lake Clifton stromatolites and are thought to have formed in much the same manner. No tiger snakes were encountered.

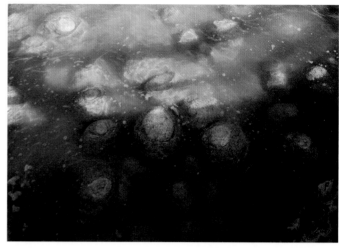

Figure 11-25. Overview of conical thrombolites forming in deeper parts of Lake Clifton.

Figure 11-26. Close-up of a conical thrombolite, Lake Clifton.

Figure 11-27. Overview of Lake Richmond, Western Australia.

Figure 11-28. Thrombolites forming along the edge of Lake Richmond.

Before returning to Perth, we made a stop at Lake Wallyungup, about five miles southwest of Rockingham. According to McNamara, the lake is fed by groundwater and is largely dry during the summer, which was the case when we were there. The stromatolites here are thrombolitic and are much larger than those of Lake Clifton or Lake Richmond, reaching heights over five feet. According to McNamara, these stromatolites are not preserved as aragonite (calcium carbonate) but as the mineral hydromagnesite (magnesium carbonate). The lake water is known to be enriched in magnesium and depleted in calcium.

Figure 11-29. Close-up of the thrombolites along the edge of Lake Richmond.

Figure 11-30. Overview of Lake Wallyungup with thrombolites in the background.

The next stop in our quest to see and photograph as many of the Western Australian stromatolites as we could find was at Lake Thetis, just north of Perth and a mile-and-a-half southeast of Cervantes. According to McNamara, the lake water is 1.3 to 1.4 times more saline than seawater. Groundwater rich in calcium bicarbonate is discharged into the lake and provides the necessary material for stromatolite growth. Also according to McNamara, "the stromatolites are formed by cyano-bacteria and diatoms." Some of the stromatolites are more than three feet in diameter with the tops eroded away. McNamara points out that another unusual feature of Lake Thetis stromatolites is the presence of branched columnar forms within the individual stromatolites. Branching of the columns in modern "stroms" is rare, but such forms were common in ancient Precambrian stromatolites.

Figure 11-31. The author providing scale to the thrombolites in Lake Wallyungup, which are very different from those at Lake Richmond and Lake Clifton.

Figure 11-32. An assemblage of stromatolites at Lake Thetis; these show reduced stromatolitic growth in their centers.

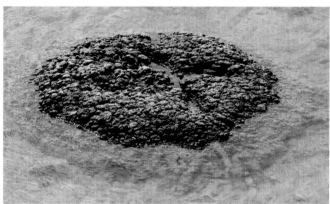

Figure 11-33. Domal stromatolites at Lake Thetis, Cervantes, Western Australia.

Figure 11-34. More stromatolitic formation at Lake Thetis, Cervantes, Western Australia. According to the sign at the preserve, laminar and thrombolitic stromatolites are growing in this lake.

We arrived at our Shark Bay destination late at night after a harrowing sixty-mile drive from Highway 1 to Denham. We were told that not many drive that stretch of road after dark because of the many emus and kangaroos that cross the highway. At sun-up the next morning we drove back down to Hamelin Pool in Shark Bay (the most spectacular location of modern "stroms"). The tide was coming in and the stromatolites were awesome. The stromatolites stretched as far as one could see and were everything I imagined, and more. One certainly had a sense of going back billions of years. On closer examination, however, birds in the air, humans on the boardwalk, fish in the sea, and even a sea snake brought us back to the present.

Over the next three days, we took several hundred photos at high and low tides, at the main reserve, and at Carbla Station. The stromatolites at Carbla Station were otherworldly, since we were probably the only people within five miles. When looking out over the vast expanse of stromatolites rising above the water in Hamelin Pool, it was easy to imagine being a witness to the earth's first stirrings of life. This sight alone made the whole trip worthwhile and was a dream come true for me.

The shallows of Hamelin Pool are formed by the vast seagrass beds making up the Fauré Sill, which blocks tidal flows into the pool and causes it to become hypersaline. The water in Hamelin Pool is twice as salty as ocean water. Animals that would normally graze on algae cannot survive these hypersaline conditions. Some experts question whether stromatolites can exist only in harsh environments that preclude grazers. Current thought and research tends to show that their existence depends on low levels of nutrients, which discourage and preclude competing organisms. (McNamara 2009, Geoscientist)

Figure 11-35. Satellite photo of Shark Bay, Western Australia. Carbla Station and Hamelin are both places where we photographed the stromatolites. Also visible is the Fauré Sill, created by vast seagrass beds that restrict tidal flow into and out of Hamelin Pool. This sill and the lack of freshwater entering the pool keep it in a hypersaline state that allows the stromatolites to flourish in Shark Bay. Shark Bay is one of only two known marine environments where stromatolites occur today; the other is Exuma Cays in the Bahamas.

Figure 11-36. Boardwalk overlooking the stromatolites in Hamelin Pool, Shark Bay, Western Australia. It wasn't until 1956 that the Shark Bay stromatolites were identified.

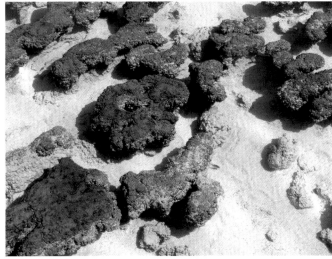

Figure 11-37. Stromatolites at high tide in Hamelin Pool. The loaf-shaped stromatolites form in the shallower parts of the pool.

Approximately 3,000–4,000 years ago, cyanobacteria began forming stromatolites in Hamelin Pool much as they did billions of years ago. They feel and look like rock, but they are very much alive. Each stromatolite has a surface consisting of living cyanobacteria. These rocks (stromatolites) are slippery when wet, as I can attest. It has been determined that some fifty-plus species of cyanobacteria live in Hamelin Pool, and some form vast cyanobacterial mats as well as stromatolites. The stromatolites of Hamelin Pool form with the sticky cyanobacteria, trapping sediments including cockleshells. These trapped sediments react with calcium carbonate in the water and form limestone layers. The limestone layers accumulate very slowly; a two-foot-high stromatolite is approximately 1,500 years old. According to an article from the 2009 World Heritage handout, the immediate Hamlin Pool environment influences their size and shape. Mushroom-shaped stromatolites form in places

Figure 11-38. Stromatolites at high tide, Hamelin Pool. A mushroom-shaped stromatolite has formed in a deeper part of the pool.

Figure 11-39. A sea snake looking for prey among the stromatolites in Hamelin Pool.

Figure 11-40. Hamelin Pool stromatolites from a water-level perspective. In the background, R. Leis walks on a beach composed of salt-tolerant Hamelin cockleshells. These shells have accumulated over the years to a depth of many feet and solidified to such an extent that they were locally quarried as building blocks.

Figure 11-41. Shark Bay stromatolites accessed through Carbla Station, which is private property and not normally open to the public. There were no signs of people, instilling a sense of going back to the beginning of life.

where they are subjected to waves and tides from different directions. Loaf-shaped stromatolites form in protected areas close to shore. Because of the need for sunlight to photosynthesize, you will not find stromatolites in Hamelin Pool at depths greater than twelve feet.

Some paleontologists note that the Shark Bay stromatolites appear to be the same as ancient stromatolites, but the shape alone does not mean that much because the environments they formed in are vastly different. Modern stromatolites often contain life forms that were not around when the Archean stromatolites formed. The introduction of this new material, such as multi-celled algae, diatoms, and other Foraminifera, changes the shape of a stromatolite. This Foraminifera is much younger than the mineralizing microorganisms that existed in the time of Precambrian stromatolites.

Present-day stromatolites show great diversity around the world—they have different shapes and forms and each hosts a wide variety of bacteria

Figure 11-42. Stromatolites in Shark Bay are extremely slow-growing. In deeper waters they may be as much as five feet tall and over 3,000 years old.

Figure 11-43 Mushroom-shaped stromatolites at low tide, Hamelin Pool, Shark Bay. The top few inches of the stromatolites consist of a bacterial mat growing in fine layers with a crown of photosynthetic bacteria that is slippery when wet.

Figure 11-44. Close-up of an approximately two-foot-high stromatolite at low tide, Hamelin Pool.

Figure 11-45. A shallower part of Hamelin Pool at low tide with more loaf-shaped stromatolites. The stromatolites on the pool edge continues for miles and as far as the eye could see.

Figure 11-46. The extensive microbial mat and stromatolite formations at Hamelin Pool. This photo also conveys the prehistoric look and feel of the place.

and archaea. Modern stromatolites also contain a variety of viruses and eukaryotes. These variations may suggest that they might represent different evolutionary stages. However, today's living stromatolites probably vary more because of their living environments. The differences in modern-day stromatolites are probably more dependent on their biology, geology, chemistry, or location than evolution.

During a May 2008 Astrobiology Science Conference in California, Malcolm Walter, professor of astrobiology, University of South Wales, Australia, and director of the Australian Center for Astrobiology (ACA), stated that he believes life began well before 3.5 billion years ago. Professor Walter says the evidence comes from stromatolites — sedimentary rocks sculpted by microbes at Shark Bay,

Australia. "Previous studies of Shark Bay stromatolites concluded the rocks were made mainly by cyanobacteria," says Walter, who has studied both modern and ancient stromatolites. But he says a team from the ACA used molecular techniques to identify genetic traces of the microbes in the stromatolites and were surprised by what they found. "The communities are far more diverse and complex than previously understood," Walter says. "There are at least 100 different species of microbes, whereas before we might have documented five or ten at the most." Walter says scientists are interested in understanding and studying modern-day stromatolites because they can shed light on the evolution of life. To quote Walter, "Stromatolites are the commonest types of fossils found in the ancient rock record, so if we

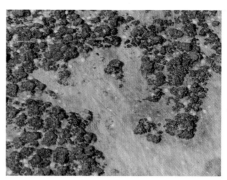

Figure 11-47. Wagon wheel tracks through the microbial mat made over sixty years ago and still plainly visible. This illustrates how fragile the Hamelin Pool ecosystem is.

Figure 11-48. A close-up of the microbial mat formation at Hamelin Pool. Note the cockleshells that eventually become incorporated into the mat. Microbial mats flourish in this hypersaline extreme environment because of the exclusion of other competing plants and animals.

Figure 11-49. Cross-section of many layers of microbial mat infused with cockleshells.

Figure 11-50. A red-capped stromatolite at Hamelin Pool that stopped growing approximately 500–1000 years ago. The red color may come from iron in the water, coloring it after it stopped growing.

understand how the modern ones form, we've got a better chance of learning about early life on earth." According to Walter, the recent findings are relevant to understanding the construction of 3.5-billion-year-old stromatolites in the Pilbara region of Western Australia—believed to be the oldest convincing evidence of life on earth. "We've tended to have a fairly simplistic interpretation of ancient microbial communities, including those that constructed ancient stromatolites," he says. The modern Shark Bay stromatolites suggest a "complex consortia" of microbes that must also have been involved in building the ancient Pilbara stromatolites, and pushes back the time when life must have first evolved. "You have to allow time for such complex communities to have evolved," Walter says. "That would suggest that life began well before 3.5 billion years ago." This makes sense to me, because if you agree that the 3.5 b.y. old Pilbara

stromatolites were formed by colonial bacteria, then single-celled bacteria that eventually colonized would have had to exist well before colonization occurred.

While these thoughts and theories about present-day stromatolites are insightful and thought provoking, for me it is enough to know that they have persisted for 3.5 billion years. The fact that these ancient structures have been around for so long, and altered the earth like they did, is truly amazing. We owe much to these simple organisms— for the oxygenation of our atmosphere and for being causal agents for Banded Iron Formations. I believe that most people, even many who are interested in fossils, do not appreciate what an impact these simple life forms have had on the earth. It is our hope that this book has conveyed a greater appreciation for stromatolites and all they have done to make Earth what it is today.

Glossary

Archaea. A domain or kingdom of single-celled organisms that are prokaryotes. These microbes have no cell nucleus or any other organelles inside their cells and can survive extreme conditions. The other domains are bacterium and eukaryotes.

Aragonite. A mineral consisting of calcium carbonate crystals, converts to calcite with geologic time, typically occurring in white seashells, stalactites, and as colorless prisms in deposits in hot springs.

Calcium bicarbonate. Also known as calcium hydrogen carbonate. Its chemical formula is Ca(HCO3)2 and exists only in aqueous solution containing ions of calcium and bicarbonate.

Calcium carbonate. $CaCO_3$ is a white powder or colorless crystalline compound found mainly in limestone, marble, and chalk; as calcite, aragonite, etc.; and in bones, teeth, shells, and plant ash. It is usually the principal cause of hard water.

Diatom. A single-celled photosynthesizing algae that has a cell wall of silica. Diatoms are among the most common types of phytoplankton, and while most are unicellular, they can exist as colonies shaped as filaments, fans, zigzags, or stars.

Eukaryote. A single-celled or multicellular organism whose cells contain a distinct membrane-bound nucleus. It belongs to the domain Eukaryota and includes protista, fungi, plants, and animals.

Filamentous cyanobacteria. A thread-like or stringy type of bacteria that obtain energy through photosynthesis.

Foraminifera. A single-celled plankton-like animal with a perforated chalky shell through which slender protrusions of protoplasm extend.

Fumarole. A hole in a volcanic region from which hot gases and vapors escape.

Hydrothermal. Relating to hot water within or on the ground's surface, pertaining to the action of hot solutions containing water or gases heated by magma within the earth's surface.

Hypersaline. A landlocked body of water that contains significant concentrations of sodium chloride or the mineral salts with saline levels surpassing that of ocean water.

Silica. A white or colorless crystalline compound SiO_2 occurring abundantly as quartz, sand, flint, agate, and many other minerals.

Sill. A submerged ridge at relatively shallow depth separating the basins of two bodies of water.

Bibliography

Alles, David L. 2012. *Stromatolites*. Western Washington University, (http://fire.biol.www.edu/trent/alles/Stromatolites.pdf).

Awramik, Stanley M. 2006. "Palaeontology: Respect for stromatolites." *Nature*, 441:700-701.

Baugh, L. Sue. 2012. *Echoes of Earth, Finding Ourselves in the Origins of the Planet*. Evanston, IL: Wild Stone Arts.

McNamara, Ken. 2009. *Stromatolites*. Perth: Western Australia Museum Publishing.

McNamara, Ken. 2009. "Stromatolites—great survivors under threat." *GeoScientist*, 19:16-22.

Reid, R. Pamela, P. T. Visscher, A. W. Decho, J. F. Stolz, B. M. Bebout, C. Dupraz, I. G. MacIntyre, H. W. Paerl, J. L. Pinckney, L. Prufert-Bebout, T. F. Steppe and D. J. DesMarais. 2000. "The role of microbes in accretion, lamination and early lithification of modern marine stromatolites." *Nature*, 406:989-992.

Reid, R. Pamela, Jamie S. Foster, Gudrun Radtke, and Stjepko Golubic. 2011. "Modern marine stromatolites of Little Darby Island, Exuma archipelago, Bahamas: Environmental setting, accretion mechanisms and role of euendoliths." *Advances in Stromatolite Geobiology*, 131:77-89. books.google.com/books?isbn=3642104142

Schopf, J. William. 1999. *Cradle of Life: The Discovery of Earth's Earliest Fossils*, Princeton, New Jersey: Princeton University Press.

Sheehan, Kathy B., David J. Patterson, Brett L. Dicks, and Joan M. Henson. 2005. *Seen and Unseen, Discovering the Microbes of Yellowstone*. Helena, Montana: Falcon Press Publishing.

Walter, Malcolm R. 2009. "The search for the earliest life on Earth." In Genes to Galaxies, edited by Adam Selinger and Anne Green. The Science Foundation for Physics within The University of Sydney.

Acknowledgments
R.J. Leis

I would like to thank the following persons who helped make this book possible.

The most important person I wish to thank is my wonderful wife, Linda. Without her help and encouragement this book would not have happened. Linda has always been there for me in all my ventures, and this one was no exception, whether it was helping to find the collecting sites or using her photography and computer skills. I would also like to thank my two daughters, Andrea and Laura. Andrea Budahn did a great job photographing many of the fossil stromatolites displayed in this book. Laura Pederson gave me the idea to write and set an example by writing her own book. Dr. Bruce Stinchcomb, my co-author, has been most patient, tolerant, and encouraging. I appreciated his willingness to answer any of my questions regardless of how basic; his geological critiques of my writing have been invaluable.

Terry McKee contributed his great artwork and illustrations. On our stromatolite collecting and photographing trips to Wyoming and Colorado, we wouldn't have gotten to some sites without him and his truck. Dan Damrow taught me much about stromatolites and sold me many of the specimens shown in this book. Barb Drealan got me interested in fossils in the first place. Tom Johnson's enduring friendship and encouragement regarding this book was much appreciated. Esther Bunch provided proofreading expertise. Tom Nash gave his time and patience in twice guiding us around the Steep Rock Mine in Atikoken, Ontario. Thank you to Terry Chase, who also appreciates stromatolites and from whom I have obtained many specimens. Tom Shearer provided close-up images of my stromatolites, especially the Mary Ellen Jasper. Gene LaBerge provided expertise, photos, and locations of material relevant to this book.

Photo credits

We extend our deep appreciation to the following for contributing photo images for this book:

Baughman, Dan: chapter 4-43a.
Berdusco, E. N.: chapter 4-25.
Budahn, Andrea M.: intro-1; chapter 1—4, 5, 6, 7, 9, 10, 14, 16, 18, 19, 20, 21, 23, 26, 27, 28, 30, 31, 32, 33, 34, 35, 36, 37; chapter 3—11, 12, 13, 14, 18, 20, 21, 23, 24, 25, 26, 27, 28, 29, 30, 32. chapter 4-16, 20, 21, 27, 43; chapter 5—7, 8, 9, 11, 13, 14, 15, 16, 17, 19, 20, 23, 24, 25, 26, 28, 33, 34, 35, 37, 38, 39, 42, 45, 46, 47, 48, 49, 54, 55, 59, 60, 61, 62, 63, 64, 66, 67, 69, 70, 71, 72, 73, 74, 81, 82, 83, 84, 85, 86, 87, 88, 89, 90, 92, 93, 94, 95, 96, 98, 100, 101, 102, 103, 106, 110, 111, 117, 119, 120, 121, 122, 123, 125, 126, 128, 129, 130, 134, 136, 137, 138, 139; chapter 6—28, 39; chapter 7—12, 14, 15; chapter 8—5, 6, 7, 8, 9, 10, 14, 15, 16, 17, 18, 19, 31, 32, 33, 34, 35, 36, 37, 38, 39, 40, 41, 42, 43, 44, 45, 46; chapter 9—2, 3, 4, 5, 10, 11, 12, 14, 15, 16, 18, 30, 31, 32, 33, 34, 35, 36, 37, 38, 39, 40, 43
Chase Studios/Terry Chase: chapter 5—21; chapter 9—17
Damrow, Cynthia: chapter 10—72
Davis, Kieran: chapter 9-19, 20
Howell, Anthony: chapter 4—22
Johnson, Tom R.: chapter 10—10, 11, 12, 66, 67
Kumar, D. C.: chapter 5—36
LaBerge, Gene L.: chapter 3—4, 10, 17
Leis, Linda A.: preface—2; chapter 1—11, 24, 39; chapter 2-12, 13; chapter 3—15, 19, 22, 31; chapter 4—17, 28, 30, 33, 34, 37, 38; chapter 5—40, 104, 127; chapter 6-30, 31; chapter 7—1, 2, 3, 4, 5, 6, 7, 8; chapter 8—1, 2, 3, 4, 25, 27, 28, 29, 30, 49, 50, 51, 65, 66, 68, 69, 78, 79, 80, 81, 82, 83, 84; chapter 9—1, 7, 8, 9, 13, 22, 23, 24, 27, 28, 29, 41, 42, 46; chapter 10—1, 4, 5, 7, 8, 9, 13, 14, 15, 16, 17, 18, 20, 21, 22, 23, 24, 25, 26, 27, 28, 29, 30, 31, 32, 33, 34, 35, 36, 37, 38, 39, 40, 41, 43, 44, 45, 46, 47, 48, 49, 50, 51, 52, 53, 54, 55, 56, 59, 60, 61, 62, 63, 64, 65, 68, 69, 69a, 70, 71, 74, 75, 79, 81, 82; chapter 11—5, 6, 7, 8, 9, 10, 11, 12, 13, 14, 16, 17, 18, 19, 20, 21, 23, 24, 25, 26, 27, 28, 29, 30, 31, 32, 33, 34, 35, 37, 38, 39, 40, 41, 42, 43, 44, 45, 46, 47, 48, 49, 50, 51
Leis, Robert J.: chapter 2—21; chapter 3—5, 6, 7, 8, 9, 16; chapter 8—48; chapter 10—2, 3, 6, 19, 42, 57, 58; chapter 9—44, 45; chapter 10—73, 76, 77, 78, 80; chapter 11—15
Lucas, Spencer G.: chapter 3—1
McKee, Terry (illustrations and reconstruction paintings): intro—2, 3. chapter 1—1, 2, 3, 8, 12, 13, 17, 22, 25, 29, 38; chapter 3—2, 3; chapter 4—1; chapter 5—5, 56, 57, 77, 91, 97, 105, 108, 115, 124
Nash, Tom: chapter 4—29, 31, 32
Reid, R. Pamela: chapter 11—1, 2, 3, 4
Riesch, Mike: chapter 5—113, 114
Savola, William: chapter 8—26, 47
Shearer, Thomas P.: preface—1; chapter 1—15, 31; chapter 5—6, 109, 131, 132, 133, 135; chapter 8—11, 12, 13, 20, 21, 22, 23, 24; chapter 9—6
Stinchcomb, Bruce L.: chapter 2—1, 2, 3, 4, 5, 6, 7, 8, 9, 10, 11, 14, 15, 16, 17, 18, 19, 20, 22, 23, 24, 25, 26, 27, 28, 29, 30, 31, 32; chapter 4—2, 3, 4, 5, 6, 7, 8, 9, 10, 11, 12, 13, 14, 15, 18, 19, 23, 24, 26, 35, 36, 39, 40, 41, 42, 44; chapter 5—3, 4, 10, 18, 22, 27, 29, 30, 31, 32, 41, 43, 44, 50, 51, 52, 53, 58, 65, 68, 75, 76, 78, 79, 80, 99, 107, 112, 116, 118; chapter 6—1, 2, 3, 4, 5, 6, 7, 8, 9, 10, 11, 12, 13, 14, 15, 16, 17, 18, 19, 20, 21, 22, 23, 24, 25, 26, 27, 29, 32, 33, 34, 35, 36, 37, 40, 41, 42, 43, 44, 45, 46; chapter 7—9, 10, 11, 13, 16, 17, 18, 19, 20, 21, 22, 23, 24; chapter 8—52, 53, 54, 55, 56, 57, 58, 59, 60, 61, 62, 63, 64, 67, 70, 71, 72, 73, 74, 75, 76, 77
Teece, Mark: chapter 9—25, 26

Index